Correcting Gender Myopia:

GENDER EQUITY, WOMEN'S WELFARE, AND THE ENVIRONMENT

DANIELLE NIERENBERG

Thomas Prugh, *Editor*

WORLDWATCH PAPER 161

September 2002

FINANCIAL SUPPORT for the Institute is provided by the Ford Foundation, the Richard & Rhoda Goldman Fund, the George Gund Foundation, the William and Flora Hewlett Foundation, The Frances Lear Foundation, the Steve Leuthold Foundation, the Charles Stewart Mott Foundation, the Curtis and Edith Munson Foundation, the John D. and Catherine T. MacArthur Foundation, the Overbrook Foundation, the David and Lucile Packard Foundation, the Surdna Foundation, Inc., the Turner Foundation, Inc., UN Environment Programme, the Wallace Global Fund, the Weeden Foundation, and the Winslow Foundation. The Institute also receives financial support from its Council of Sponsors members—Adam and Rachel Albright, Tom and Cathy Crain, and Robert Wallace and Raisa Scriabine—and from the many other friends of Worldwatch.

THE WORLDWATCH PAPERS provide in-depth, quantitative, and qualitative analysis of the major issues affecting prospects for a sustainable society. The Papers are written by members of the Worldwatch Institute research staff and reviewed by experts in the field. Regularly published in five languages, they have been used as concise and authoritative references by governments, nongovernmental organizations, and educational institutions worldwide. For a partial list of available Papers, see back pages.

Table of Contents

Figures, Tables, and Boxes

ACKNOWLEDGEMENTS: This paper is based on the *State of the World 2002* chapter "Rethinking Population, Improving Lives," by Robert Engelman, Brian Halweil, and Danielle Nierenberg. I am grateful to Mercedes Guichardo, Margaret Greene, Stan Bernstein, Jodi Jacobson, Rachel Kyte, Nada Chaya, and Richard P. Cincotta for sharing both research and their experience. I am particularly grateful to Robert Engelman, who provided guidance and encouragement throughout the writing of both the chapter and paper. Mia MacDonald, Lori Ashford, Stacy Cordery, and Joyce Nierenberg were kind enough to provide thoughtful criticisms and suggestions on various drafts of this paper.

Many at Worldwatch were indispensable in producing this paper. I am thankful for the input of Brian Halweil, Chris Bright, Anne Platt McGinn, Molly O'Meara Sheehan, Radhika Sarin, Gary Gardner, and Richard Bell. Interns Meghan Crimmins and Arunima Dhar lent their creativity and expertise and Research Librarian Lori Brown helped me track down information and gave me encouragement. Linda Starke edited the *State of the World 2002* chapter that later developed into this paper and Senior Editor Tom Prugh, the paper editor, made sure my i's were dotted and t's crossed and that jargon was replaced with easy-to-understand language. Behind the scenes, Art Director Lyle Rosbotham transformed text and raw data into the paper you now hold, and Leanne Mitchell and Susan Finkelpearl ensured that a wide audience would be exposed to my research.

DANIELLE NIERENBERG is a Staff Researcher at Worldwatch Institute who studies sustainable agriculture, meat production, animal welfare, food safety, and gender and population. Her work includes two major articles for *World Watch* magazine, "Toxic Fertility"(on the disruption of the nitrogen cycle, in the March/April 2001 issue), and "Dim Vision" (on the Bush administration's environmental agenda, July/August 2001). Danielle worked with Research Associate Brian Halweil to produce the issue brief, "How Now Mad Cow," a commentary on agriculture as a conduit for animal and human diseases that was printed in the *International Herald Tribune* and several other print and online publications. With Robert Engelman and Brian Halweil, she also co-authored a chapter for *State of the World 2002*, "Rethinking Population, Improving Lives." Danielle covered human migration for the 2001 edition of *Vital Signs*, and population, mental health, food safety, and gender-based violence for *Vital Signs 2002*, the Institute's annual survey of environmental and social trends. She is currently working with Brian on a project concerning global meat production and consumption.

Danielle has a master's degree in Agriculture, Food, and Environment from the School of Nutrition Science and Policy at Tufts University in Boston. Her bachelor's degree, in Environmental Policy, is from Monmouth College in Monmouth, Illinois.

A Woman's Life

Mercedes Guichardo begins her day, like many of the 4 million other women in the Dominican Republic, with one thought on her mind: water. Demand for water far outstrips supply in San Francisco de Macoris, the island's fifth most populous *pueblo* (city), Mercedes' home. Running water is a luxury few can afford, but Mercedes is considered lucky by Dominican standards because she has access to a communal faucet near her house. There, the water trickles out three or four times a week. But the half-dozen or so families who depend on it are never sure when it will come; sometimes it starts flowing at 4 a.m., other days it doesn't come until late afternoon. For women like Mercedes, who trek to the free trade zone factories during the week, getting enough water for bathing, cooking, housekeeping, and drinking is a constant struggle.[1]

Mercedes was born and raised in San Francisco de Macoris, and during her 41 years she has seen her town become one of the largest in the country. Just since 1993, the population of the city has grown by 23 percent, from 108,000 to more than 133,000 people. And as the city has grown, Mercedes has watched her own life change dramatically. She has been a daughter, a student, a wife, a mother, head of a household, and most recently a member of the paid labor force. Some of these roles she anticipated, others were thrust upon her because of her status as a woman.[2]

Mercedes was fortunate enough to both want and plan her pregnancies. Although she had two miscarriages and postpartum problems after her youngest child was born, her three children have all survived past the critical five-year mark. What Mercedes didn't anticipate was being a single mother. One-quarter of all households in the Dominican Republic are headed by women, but they receive little support from government or non-governmental agencies. Despite the economic hardship of being without a partner, Mercedes feels lucky to no longer be married to a physically and emotionally abusive man, even if he was the breadwinner in the family. Since the divorce—surprisingly, not rare in this Catholic nation—she has depended on other means to support herself and the children, including sewing clothing at a foreign-owned factory, cooking for a local restaurant, cleaning houses in the wealthy part of town, and getting loans from Dominican Yorks (relatives either currently living in *Nueva York* or who have recently returned to the Dominican Republic after earning money in the United States).[3]

Mercedes' life is not so different from the lives of millions of other intelligent and hardworking women around the world. Although they speak different languages, pray to different gods, or have different colored skin, they all share the burden of gender inequity. For some, discrimination against their sex is as familiar as the geography of their native country, preventing many from dreaming of a life different from their mothers' or grandmothers'. Others struggle to secure the rights they know they are due, but that remain out of reach: the power to decide when to have sex, whether to have children, and how many; an education equal to that of boys; representation in government; a clean environment; and equal pay for equal work. When such inequities exist in developing and developed nations alike, women have little say in what course their lives will take, and the results can be devastating to their health, the health of their children, and the health of the planet.

At international conferences throughout the 1990s, from Rio de Janeiro to Vienna and from Cairo to Beijing, women's health and human rights slowly but steadily made their way onto the international agenda. For example, at the United Nations Conference on Environment and Development (also known as the Earth Summit) in Rio in 1992, women's groups from developing as well as industrial countries lobbied for social change. Agenda 21, the plan of action that emerged from the conference, called for women's "full participation" in sustainable development; improvement in women's status, access to education, and income; and attention to the needs of women as well as men for access to reproductive health services, including family planning "education, information and means." This set the stage for the International Conference on Population and Development (ICPD) in Cairo in 1994, where the Programme of Action affirmed that reproductive and sexual health is a basic human right. A year later in Beijing, the Fourth World Conference on Women reaffirmed women's rights and their equal participation in all spheres of society as a prerequisite for human development. Thanks in large part to the involvement of women themselves, often acting together in nongovernmental organizations (NGOs) and coalitions, women are less likely to be seen as passive recipients of population and reproductive health programs but instead as full participants in a world where all people, including the young, are free to express their sexuality freely, safely, and responsibly.

These advances are overdue and welcome, but insufficient. Gender myopia—blindness to inequities between women and men—still distorts environmental, economic, and health policies in all nations. Today, almost a full decade after the 1994 International Conference on Population and Development in Cairo, governments, development agencies, and even some nongovernmental organizations remain resolutely patriarchal. Despite the widespread belief that women have come a long way in improving their social and economic status, they still face many of the same obstacles. In some cases these problems have become even more formidable.

Many women—and not only in the less-developed world—do not have the option that Mercedes had of planning pregnancies and spacing births. Nearly two out of every five women who learn they are pregnant wish they had waited at least a couple of years before giving birth again, if at all. And there are probably thousands of women and men who would prefer to remain childless, but become parents because of pressure from their families or society. There is no question that if all pregnancies in all nations could be the happy outcomes of women and men making earnest commitments to be parents, population growth would slow even more rapidly than it is today.[4]

Anyone who seeks to fathom the future interaction between humans and the natural world must consider population change a dominant force on the human side of that relationship. There is more to population and related policies, however, than the numbers and distribution of people. Demographers, social scientists, and politicians increasingly recognize the connections between human numbers and behavior, relationships, health care, and especially the circumstances and status of women all over the world. Evolving from decades of demographic research and field experience, "population" policy now embraces a diversity of efforts to improve the health, livelihoods, and capacities of women at each stage of their lives, as daughters, students, wives, mothers, resource managers, and community leaders. "Population," says former United Nations Population Fund director Nafis Sadik, "is essentially about gender equality and equity."[5]

The concept of reproductive health has also changed to encompass much more than preventing pregnancy through birth control. It now includes sex education, access to contraceptives, information about sexually transmitted diseases, infertility, and all other matters relating to the reproductive system. The United Nations defines reproductive health as "a state of complete physical, mental, and social well-being...in all matters related to the reproductive system, and its functions and processes. Reproductive health therefore implies that people are able to have a satisfying and safe sex life and they have the capability to reproduce and the freedom to decide if, when, and how often to do so."[6]

The population and reproductive health fields have traditionally focused on women, even though men have historically exerted more control over when to have sex and whether to use contraception. Providing education and health services for girls and women can hardly address all needs, however, until boys and men are engaged in efforts to improve unequal gender relations. Mercedes' son Jonathon, for example, is growing up like many others in a *machismo* culture where concepts of manliness often include having unprotected sex with multiple partners, or beating wives and girlfriends. Luckily, in many places those attitudes are changing. "Increasingly, men—and especially younger men—see the opportunity for egalitarian relationships between men and women as a boon," the late family expert Perdita Huston wrote, "a fortunate trend that may allow them to become more involved in family life and less beholden to strict and restrictive gender roles."[7]

In considering the links between population, environmental change, and gender equality, a near revolution in thinking among demographers, family planning advocates, NGOs, and politicians has occurred since the Earth Summit in 1992. It is increasingly clear that the long-term future of environmental and human health—and, critically, the global population peak—is bound up in the rights and capacities of youth, especially young women, to control their own lives and destinies. Societies in rich nations and poor need a new kind of vision that acknowledges the long-term implications of current relations between women and men and sees the critical role gender plays in human development. As long as girls and women are thought to be less able than boys and men to navigate human experience and forge their own paths in life, population policy will always be flawed. On the other hand, when girls go to school free of fear of violence and sexual coercion and when women reach economic, social, and political parity with men, they have fewer children and give birth later on average than their mothers did. Assuming good access to health and family planning services, fertility almost invariably declines to or below replacement level. That slows the growth of population.

The centrality of women's status to our demographic future also produces discomfort among people to whom it implies that interest in slowing population growth might turn women into instruments for some "larger" purpose, or into commodities to be counted and valued for their reproductive decisions and actions. Those who work to slow the growth of population and those who work for women's parity with men sometimes are the same people, aiming for many of the same interim objectives: access to comprehensive and integrated reproductive health care, an end to the gender gap in education and in economic opportunities, the elimination of violence against women. Certain changes are essential for women themselves from a human rights perspective and will simultaneously contribute to broader improvements in population trends and in human and environmental welfare.

Population Trends, Causes, and Consequences

For most of human history, parents averaged two children who survived to become parents themselves. We know this by the simple observation that the human population grew very slowly until relatively recently. The key word here is "survived." Although some women practiced herbal and other means of contraception, most undoubtedly had many babies that did not survive long. Until recently, death rates among infants and children were so high that population growth was episodic and localized rather than consistent and global.[8]

With the advent of better nutrition and basic public health—hand washing, sanitation, immunization, and antibiotics—enough people survived infancy and childhood by the nineteenth and twentieth centuries to boost population growth to unprecedented rates. The Earth's population rose from a billion people around 1800 to 1.6 billion in 1900, 2.5 billion by 1950, and then 6.1 billion by 2000. Sometime in the 1960s the global rate of population growth peaked and began to decline— from 2.1 percent a year to just under 1.3 percent today— although the still-growing population base meant that annual additions to human numbers continued increasing until recently. Even today, the planet adds about 77 million people

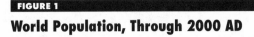

World Population, Through 2000 AD

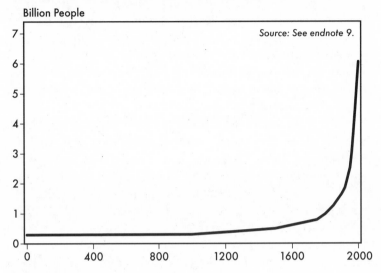

Billion People

Source: See endnote 9.

each year, the equivalent of 10 New York Cities.[9] (See Figure 1.)

But the rate of population growth is slowing as ideas about women's status and childbearing change and as access to contraception improves around the world. If average family size had not declined from the level in 1960 and death rates had stayed the same, more than 8 billion people would be alive today instead of 6.2 billion. In 2002, the United Nations Population Division revised its long-held prediction of a population of 10 billion people by the end of the century. Demographers now believe that the total population will be at or around 9 billion people by 2050. According to this new scenario, total world population will begin to shrink over the next hundred years. For many wealthy nations, family size has decreased enough to one day reverse population growth. In a few countries, such as Italy and Russia, population is declining already. In much of Europe and in Japan, use of birth control rose so rapidly from the 1970s through the 1990s that fertility fell well below the replacement level of 2.1 children per woman; eventually, such low fertility will end population growth in these nations as well. (Some governments fear this trend. In Japan, the government has advocated a "structural reform in lifestyle" that urges Japanese women to "work less and have more babies." But others argue that such trends are simply the byproduct of lower infant mortality, longer life spans, better educational and economic opportunities for women, and so on, and that changes in tax, social security, and immigration policies can ease the transition to new population sizes and structures.)[10]

Each year, about 12 million people reach their sixtieth birthdays. According to the United Nations, the global decline in fertility and the increase in life spans means that, for the first time in human history, the old will outnumber the young by 2050. The majority of older people in the world are already women, an imbalance that is likely to worsen. Among the oldest (aged 80 and above) there are two to five times as many women as men, and aging is not gender-neutral. In a number of places, such as India and South Africa, a combination of factors (migration, the HIV/AIDS crisis, urbanization, the deterioration of traditional family structures, and the tendency of women to outlive their partners) has forced many older women into poverty and isolation. The United Nations predicts that more women than men will live in poor health or with a disability as the population ages. Women are more likely to suffer from chronic disabling conditions, such as diabetes, Alzheimer's disease, hypertension, and osteoporosis, which now cripples some 200 million women worldwide. For these and other reasons, women's generally higher life expectancies do not equate to higher quality of life with old age.[11]

Even as the human population ages and the growth rate slows, population decline is anything but imminent for most countries. Average national fertility rates are at replacement level or above in more than two-thirds of the world's nations. In the world's 48 least-developed countries, population is projected to triple by 2050. In 57 more nations, the population could double. For example, the current population of Nigeria (about 120 million) is expected to grow to between 237 million and 325 million by mid-century. The number of people living on the entire continent of Africa is projected to more than double—from 840 million to between 1.7 billion and 2.3 billion—over the same period. South Central Asia (including India, Pakistan, Bangladesh, and Afghanistan) could more than double its current population of 1.5 billion. Roughly half of the world's population is under the age of 25, with all or most of their reproductive years ahead of them and little guidance or help from their parents or governments on healthy sexuality and reproduction. There can be no guarantee of a peak in world population this century without major commitments from governments to provide family planning and related services to those who seek them. Yet such commitments are anything but certain.[12]

(The stark differences between wealthy and poor nations in population trends create the conditions for a widening flow of people, increasingly women, across international borders in coming decades. An estimated 185 million people—3 out of every 100 people on the planet—already live outside their countries of birth. Between 1985 and 1990, the population of international migrants grew about 50 percent faster than world population as a whole, and given the greater migration of the 1990s and the slowdown in world population growth, it is likely that the gap has grown much wider. In the late 1980s, most migration was from one developing country to another, but in the future the South-to-North axis could dominate migration.[13] See Box 1 on pages 14 and 15.)

Despite population growth in developing countries, the overwhelming influence on human population worldwide is the fulfillment of parental intentions to postpone pregnancies and have smaller families. In the early 1960s women averaged five children each worldwide, six or more in developing countries. By 2000, these numbers had fallen by roughly half, in part because contraceptive usage multiplied sixfold from 10 percent of couples worldwide in 1960 to 60 percent in 2000. These changes are indicators of a demographic revolution that continues today.[14]

Demographers and population policy analysts increasingly recognize the health and circumstances of women to be among

BOX 1

Measures of Migration

In June 2000, 58 illegal Chinese immigrants were discovered in a nearly airless truck carrying a shipment of tomatoes from England to Belgium. Only four survived the 18-hour journey. The next summer, immigration agents patrolling the U.S.-Mexico border found the bodies of 14 Mexicans dead from dehydration, adding to the typical death toll of more than 350 illegal migrants each year. Since migration generally involves great personal risk and expense, given the choice most people would rather stay where they are—close to family, familiar places, and others who speak their language. But the larger the gap between people's current quality of life and that which they believe they can attain in a new land, the more motivation they have to leave. Refugees—migrants forced from their homes by armed conflict or political upheaval—often have little choice but to cross borders.

Among the nations that send the most migrants are China and India. Every year more than 400,000 Chinese leave for other countries and 50,000 Indians migrate to the United States, Australia, the United Kingdom, and Canada. At the other end, the two regions of the world that receive the most immigrants are North America and Western Europe. Migration has become a deeply sensitive topic in both regions, especially in the wake of the terrorist attacks on the World Trade Center and the Pentagon in 2001. On the one hand, employers and national economies benefit from the generally inexpensive labor that immigrants offer and societies benefit from cultural diversity unknown to previous generations. On the other hand, migrants make convenient targets for those fearful about the accelerating pace of change increasing congestion, or about foreigners stealing jobs. In the United States, new fears about terrorism may add to this tension.

Roughly half of the world's migrants are now women, creating a feminization of migration. In the past, men left rural villages to look for work in cities. Now many women are forced to make the same journey, and wind up working in factories, *maquiladoras*, *zonas francas* and other foreign-owned textile and assembly plants that dot Mexico, Central America, and the Caribbean, or as domestic servants. Their specific needs have received little attention, and they are particularly vulnerable to discrimination and physical or sexual abuse by employers or family members. Paid less in the workplace than male workers and lacking the same rights, some of these mostly very young women are forced into prostitution and other illicit activities in order to survive. In fact, an estimated 4 million women and girls are bought and sold worldwide

Box 1 *(continued)*

each year. Traffickers often target families hit by bad harvests and unemployment, promising to find work and schooling for their daughters in the city. Most of these young women and girls become prostitutes; at least 10,000 enter the commercial sex trade in Thailand each year and roughly 7,000 Nepali girls are trafficked into India annually for prostitution.

Migration can help raise the standard of living, not only for the migrants themselves but for the family members they leave behind. Remittances— the earnings that migrant workers send to their families back home—are an increasingly important part of the economies of developing nations. In Senegal, as much as 80 percent of household budgets comes from remittances, and in the Dominican Republic, remittances exceed the value of the country's exports by 50 percent.

Despite these economic benefits for migrants and their families, countries that migrants leave undergo a "brain drain" as their most talented members seek education or employment elsewhere. The World Bank estimates that during the 1990s, some 23,000 academics from Africa alone emigrated each year in search of better working conditions.

Male out-migration from *campos* and rural villages to urban areas can increase both female workload and environmental degradation. According to a report by the Population Reference Bureau, women's physical work burden doubled in three villages in Nepal when the men moved to the city for work. This was especially true for women with no grown sons to help them farm the land and perform physically demanding tasks that are considered taboo for women, such as plowing. In Ghana, an absent male workforce has meant that nearby fields that should have been left fallow for a few years are now overused, because gender-role specialization and lack of assistance from agricultural extension agents has left the women without the necessary farming knowledge and skills. As a result, soil erosion has increased and yields have declined.

Pressures to migrate and opposition to continued immigration are both likely to mount as population density increases and the availability of critical natural resources decreases. Ultimately, each nation must decide how many people to welcome and under what circumstances. Some nations, cities, and communities—especially those without adequate renewable water supplies—may take measures to discourage further in-migration.

Source: See endnote 13.

the strongest determinants of how many children parents have. An estimated 125 million women worldwide do not want to be pregnant but are not using any type of contraception. Millions more women (survey research has not produced a precise number) would like to avoid pregnancy but are using contraception improperly, in many cases because of misinformation about what would be the best method for them. Overall, the UN Population Fund estimates, 350 million women worldwide lack access to a range of contraceptive services. But when women's education, opportunities, and status begin to approach those of men, their economic and health conditions improve. As a result (assuming good access to family planning services), they have fewer children, and the children arrive later in the mothers' lives.[15]

A major contributor to later pregnancies and lower fertility is at least six or seven years of schooling. When girls manage to stay in school this long, what they learn about basic health, sexuality, and their own prospects in the world tends to encourage them to marry and become pregnant later in life and to have smaller families. In Egypt, for example, only 5 percent of women who stayed in school past the primary level had children while still in their teens, while over half of women with no schooling became teenage mothers. In high-fertility countries, women who have some secondary education typically have two, three, or four children fewer in their lifetimes than otherwise similar women who have never been to school.[16]

Educating girls and women also gives them higher self-esteem, greater decisionmaking power within the family, more confidence to participate fully in community affairs, and the ability to one day become educated mothers who pass on their knowledge to their own daughters and sons. Mercedes' two daughters, Gina and Gisselle, expect to not only graduate from high school, but if they can get scholarships they might even go to university, a choice their mother never had. [17]

Unfortunately, millions of young girls will not complete the fourth grade. (In the least developed nations of the world, only a little more than half of girls stay in school after grade 4). Although the gender gap in education has started to close, there are still many girls who will never sit in a classroom or open a book. An estimated 559 million women in the world are illiterate and they make up more than two-thirds of the world's total population of people that cannot read. Although literacy rates worldwide improved overall during the 1990s, they worsened slightly for women.[18]

Moreover, despite some halting progress in international and national commitments to support women's rights, women are still much less likely than men to complete secondary school, hold a paying job, or sit in a legislature or parliament. "Most political parties," says Andrew Johnson of the Inter-Parliamentary Union, "are run by men, for men." (See Table 1 on pages 18 and 19, and Figure 2 on page 20.) Economies and societies generally undervalue women's work, from the household to the farm, the factory, and the office. Women typically work longer hours than men—nurturing children, caring for elders, maintaining homes, farming, and hauling wood and water home from distant sources. This labor is largely invisible to economists and policymakers, but by some estimates it amounts to one-third of the world's economic production. And in all nations women still earn only two-thirds to three-fourths of what men earn for comparable work.[19] (See Figure 3 on page 21.)

For years economists have debated the relationship between demographic and economic change without reaching any consensus, in part because population growth operates in different ways in different countries and times, making it difficult to untangle cause and effect. However, according to economist Nancy Birdsall, various country-level studies confirm that high fertility increases absolute poverty levels by skewing the distribution of resources against the poor and slowing economic growth. Some government officials of developing countries are also willing to acknowledge that large and growing populations hamper economic development. In the Philippines, for example, economic planning secretary Dante Canlas announced last year that the country's new administration would act to slow population growth despite the opposition of the Catholic Church there. Noting the nation's rapid pop-

TABLE 1

Gender Disparities in Four Social Spheres

Sphere	Description
Education	Girls account for 60 percent of the 130 million children without access to primary education. In 22 African and 9 Asian nations, school enrollment for girls is less than 80 percent that of boys, and only 52 percent of girls in the least developed nations stay in school after grade 4. In sub-Saharan Africa and South Asia—where access to higher education is difficult for both men and women—only between 2 and 7 women per 1,000 (compared with between 4 and 11 men) attend high school and college.
Economics	In most regions, women-headed households are much more vulnerable to poverty than male-headed ones. Single-mother households in the United States have 18 percent of American children but one-third of the children living in poverty. Women make up 40 percent of the global workforce, but earn on average two-thirds to three-fourths as much as men. Women's "invisible" work (such as housekeeping and child care) is rarely included in economic accounting, although it has been valued at about one-third of the world's economic production. Women account for 5 percent of the most senior staff of the 500 largest corporations in the United States. At the International Monetary Fund, 11 percent of the economists are women, and women occupy just 15 percent of managerial positions.
Politics	Women's representation continues to increase in all nations, but women are still vastly underrepresented at all levels of government as well as in international institutions. Of the 190 heads of state and heads of government, only 11 are female. Worldwide, women hold just 14 percent of seats in parliaments. At the United Nations, women made up only 21 percent of the senior management in 1999. While Nordic nations have the highest percentage of women in parliament (40 percent of the seats in the lower and upper houses) women hold just 16 percent of parliamentary seats in the Americas and a scant 4 percent in Arab states. Only in nine countries is the share of women in the national parliament at 30 percent or above. In mid-2001, at least six countries—Djibouti, Kuwait, Palau, Tonga, Tuvalu, and Vanuatu—did not have a single woman in their legislatures.

Table 1 *(continued)*

Civic Freedom	In nations as diverse as Botswana, Chile, Namibia, and Swaziland, married women are under the permanent guardianship of their husbands and have no right to manage property (women's rights for divorce are also widely constrained). Husbands in Bolivia, Guatemala, and Syria can restrict a wife's choice to work outside the home. In some Arab nations, a wife must obtain her husband's consent in order to get a passport.

Source: See endnote 19.

ulation growth, Canlas expressed concern that "high fertility in the rural areas is exported into the urban areas and rural poverty gets transformed into urban poverty."[20]

Recent evidence suggests that under some conditions falling fertility and slower population growth can powerfully boost some economies. A number of countries in East and Southeast Asia, for example, invested strongly in health—including mother and child health care and family planning services—in the 1970s, specifically hoping that smaller families would produce economic and developmental dividends. These governments also committed themselves to education and the support of growing industries that promised to be major employers. The strategies worked. Having fewer children meant that parents could invest more in their children's schooling and health. Studies indicate, in general, that as average family size declines, savings increase, and household savings are among the major sources of internal investment in developing countries. Harvard economists recently calculated that between 1965 and 1990 the slowing of population growth accounted for as much as one-third of the rapid growth in per capita income in East Asian countries like South Korea and Taiwan.[21]

Rapid population growth can put an enormous strain on governments and other institutions. From schools and hospitals to low-cost housing and waterworks, growing numbers of people generate a larger demand for public services—a demand that ineffectual or incompetent governments often cannot meet. The rapid expansion of school-age populations, for

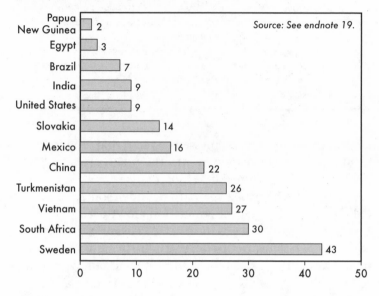

FIGURE 2

Percent of Parliamentary Seats Held by Women, Selected Countries, 2001

Source: See endnote 19.

Country	Percent
Papua New Guinea	2
Egypt	3
Brazil	7
India	9
United States	9
Slovakia	14
Mexico	16
China	22
Turkmenistan	26
Vietnam	27
South Africa	30
Sweden	43

instance, puts tremendous pressure on nations—especially those struggling to meet existing educational needs—to train more teachers and build more schools. In sub-Saharan Africa, where only 56 percent of people are literate and only one in twenty benefits from secondary education, the number of school-age children is projected to expand by over 30 percent in the next three decades. Without additional investments in education, today's average student-teacher ratio of 39 to 1 in sub-Saharan Africa will balloon to 54 to 1 by 2040.[22]

These demands converge in the mushrooming urban centers of the developing world, which are projected to be home within a few decades to virtually all future population growth. Many of these cities have doubled in population just over the past 12 to 15 years. One analysis found that young children in the largest cities of Latin America, North Africa, and Asia were less likely than children in smaller cities to have received health care or schooling and were more likely to be

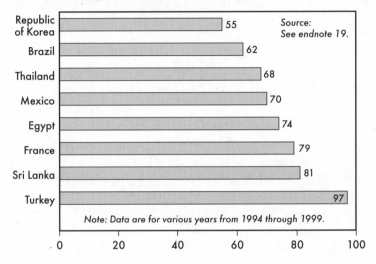

FIGURE 3

Women's Wages as a Percentage of Men's Wages in Manufacturing, Selected Countries

Republic of Korea — 55

Brazil — 62

Thailand — 68

Mexico — 70

Egypt — 74

France — 79

Sri Lanka — 81

Turkey — 97

Source: See endnote 19.

Note: Data are for various years from 1994 through 1999.

0   20   40   60   80   100

suffering from diarrhea because of a lack of clean drinking water, safe food, and sanitation. The most rapidly growing cities in Latin America and Africa suffered from the highest levels of infant and child mortality. Long-term population growth rates in excess of 5 percent a year raised the odds of infant mortality by 24 percent in North Africa and Asia, by 28 percent in Latin America and the Caribbean, and by 42 percent in tropical Africa. In the Dominican Republic, where Mercedes scrapes by week after week to raise her children and where infant and maternal mortality rates are the second highest in the Caribbean, moving to the island's rapidly growing cities might not raise the quality of life the way it once did.[23]

According to Thoraya Obaid, executive director of the UN Population Fund, reducing population growth is essential to fighting poverty and increasing human security. Demographic bulges in young age groups, for instance, may precipitate social upheaval or international aggression. "If we do not slow population growth," says Obaid, "we're only going to increase the number of people who are under the poverty

line, who are frustrated, who have no employment, no future."
Along similar lines, researchers have argued that population-
related scarcities of natural resources can also fuel conflict, especially when the needs of dense and rapidly growing populations
strain weak institutions.[24]

Revolutionizing Reproductive Health

In 1994, representatives from international institutions,
national governments, and NGOs gathered in Cairo at the
International Conference on Population and Development
(ICPD). They sketched a vision of a world in which population
stablization and sustainable development are among the many
outcomes of policies and programs that put individuals, especially women and young people, in control of their own pro-
ductive and reproductive lives. This was a breakthrough event,
bringing to policymakers and the public an intellectual revolution that had been brewing for years within the population
and women's health movements. The consensus among governments paved the way for a new people-centered, and ultimately much more effective, way to craft human development
and population policies.[25]

Through the lens of Cairo, a stable or gradually declining population can be seen as a helpful side benefit of efforts
that improve women's lives. That is, greater access to health
care and education not only yields personal and community
benefits, it also has the effect of reducing the size of families,
raising the average age of first pregnancy, and reducing the
number of children women feel they must have. Participants
from nearly every country gathered in Cairo and agreed to
adopt precisely this strategy for addressing population change—
framing population as an issue of people, especially their
capacities and their rights, more than numbers. Such thinking
went a long way toward reconciling tensions among ecologists,
demographers, and feminists regarding the causes and conse-
quences of high fertility rates and population growth.

The capacity to plan, prevent, and postpone pregnancy is essential to reproductive health, reducing maternal and child deaths, and setting the stage for women and men to manage their own sexuality and reproduction. There is much more to this aspect of health, however, than family planning alone. According to Jodi Jacobson of the Center for Health and Gender Equity, in order to address unwanted fertility, HIV/AIDS, and the whole range of women's reproductive needs and concerns, health care systems need to be sensitive to certain realities women face on a daily basis. These realities include fear of violence from partners or family members, restrictive cultural or religious traditions, and limited opportunities for education and work. For example, many women cannot negotiate contraceptive use with their partners nor can they secure contraceptives to use in secret because of lack of financial autonomy. Challenges of this sort confront women in developing and rich countries alike. For instance, two useful new contraceptives—a skin patch and a vaginal ring that each release contraceptive hormones—are not likely to be available to some 6.5 million young and poor women served by public clinics in the United States. Although these new methods might help to address the 49-percent rate of unplanned pregnancy in the United States, their expense prevents family planning and reproductive health clinics from dispensing them widely.[26]

Young people in all regions of the world face special challenges of their own related to reproductive health—such as the lack of sexual education in schools and the inability to talk to their parents about sex—whether or not they are sexually active. At the ICPD, and even more so at the conference's five-year review in New York in 1999, people in their teens and early twenties expressed their wish to be recognized and included in population and reproductive health policies and to be agents of change for implementing those initiatives.[27]

"Wait until you're older" is hardly helpful advice for the millions of adolescents already having sex or preparing to enter into intimate relationships. Yet the Bush administration's statements on the reproductive needs of youth during the UN Special Session on Children in May 2002, and its later decision to eliminate U.S. funding to the United Nations Population Fund, gravely set back efforts to provide reproductive health services to young women and men. The United States built an unusual alliance with the Vatican, Iran, and Iraq, insisting that conference documents not refer to abortion, or even include the word "services" when referring to reproductive health, because it was said to imply medical intervention after pregnancy. According to the U.S. Secretary of Health and Human Services Tommy Thompson, abstinence is the best defense and "only sure way of avoiding sexually transmitted disease, premature pregnancy, and the social and personal difficulties attendant to nonmarital sexual activity." In July, the U.S. government awarded grants totalling $27.7 million to churches, schools, and health centers to promote sexual abstinence prior to marriage. Under the law, the grants may not be used to educate youth about birth control. By 2003, President Bush hopes to increase spending for the abstinence-only campaign to $138 million.[28]

However, research in several countries has demonstrated that access to sound information and guidance on sexuality and reproduction helps young people postpone sexual activity and avoid infection and pregnancy when they do become sexually active. The young need adult guidance and support, as well as access to safe and effective contraception and reproductive health services, in order to protect themselves from violence, unplanned pregnancies, and infection from HIV/AIDS and other sexually transmitted diseases. They also need the self-confidence to say no to unwanted sex or to insist that their sexual partners use contraception.[29]

While the mere presence of contraceptive options is hardly sufficient to change women's lives and world population trends, without that access even the most highly motivated women and couples are unlikely to be sexually active for long without a pregnancy. Lack of access to services, lack of knowledge, and opposition of family members are among the most commonly cited reasons for not using contraception. Prohibitively high costs—in some sub-Saharan African nations, condoms and other birth control measures absorb 20 percent of

FIGURE 4

Contraceptive Use and Live Births Per Woman in 133 Countries

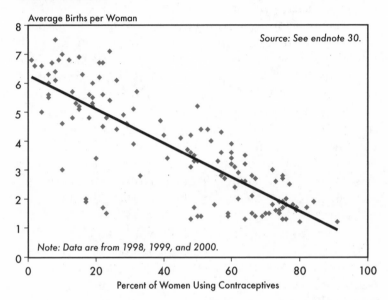

Average Births per Woman

Source: See endnote 30.

Note: Data are from 1998, 1999, and 2000.

Percent of Women Using Contraceptives

the average couple's income—also keep many women from taking action to prevent pregnancy. The correlation is straightforward: where contraceptive use in the world is high, families are smaller. (See Figure 4.) In Angola, Chad, and Afghanistan, for example, fewer than one in twenty couples uses contraception, and family size is nearly seven children per woman. In Italy, in contrast, contraceptive prevalence exceeds 90 percent and average fertility stands at 1.2 children per woman, close to the lowest fertility level in the world.[30]

If contraception were simply a means of slowing population growth, it is unlikely that most of the world's sexually active couples would be using it. The capacity to experience sex and sexuality without fear of becoming a parent is among the most liberating aspects of contemporary life, especially for women. By one analysis, the influx of women into U.S. medical, law, and other professional graduate schools in the 1970s was in large part a product of widespread availability and popularity of the oral contraceptive pill starting late in the 1960s. In developing countries, women often credit family planning for new opportunities to earn an income, pursue an education, or participate more actively in civic life.[31]

Family planning also directly improves health, especially for mothers but also for their infants and children. In developing countries, children are significantly more likely to die before their fifth birthday if they are born fewer than two years after their next older sibling, whereas a gap of four years or more between births raises infant and child survival chances above the average. Mothers themselves are more likely to survive childbearing if they use family planning to have fewer children, as it gives their bodies time to recover between each birth. And healthy mothers mean healthy infants who are more likely to survive than children whose mothers die before the child's first birthday.[32]

In recognition of the multiple benefits of family planning, most developing countries in the last 40 years have launched programs to subsidize or otherwise make more widely available sterilization, condoms, pills, injectable contraceptives, intrauterine devices, and other methods of avoiding pregnancy. By one analysis, the international family planning movement can take credit for just under half the decline in birth rates since 1960, with cultural and social change accounting for the rest. One interesting glimpse of the impact of government-sponsored family planning programs on national fertility comes from a comparison of six nations—Bangladesh, Ghana, India, Mexico, South Korea, and Zimbabwe—with strong programs begun before 1980. In each case, the use of contraception rose fairly continuously, with attendant declines in average family size that have helped slow the growth of world population appreciably. For example, after the Zimbabwean government launched its program in 1968, contraceptive use jumped from just 5 percent of the population in 1975 to 50 percent by 1993.[33]

The international community can help to close gaps where government provision of family planning and reproductive health services is constrained by tight budgets, debt, entrenched bureaucracies, or narrow political conflicts. Many industrial countries have contributed funds and technical expertise to such programs. Nongovernmental sources also shoulder a heavy load. Private U.S. foundation expenditures may now rival official U.S. overseas assistance for family planning. In Bangladesh, one-quarter of reproductive health services—including education and birth control—comes from nongovernmental groups. In Colombia, an affiliate of the International Planned Parenthood Federation called Profamilia provides more than 60 percent of family planning services.[34]

Still, the gap between the need for contraception and its availability in developing countries is particularly worrisome, because reproductive health resources appear to be entering a period of scarcity. Two waves are reaching shore simultaneously and reinforcing each other. First, the largest generation of young people in human history—1.7 billion people aged 10 to 24, projected to approach 1.8 billion by 2015—is now reaching reproductive age. The number of women already aged 15 to 49 is at an all-time high at 1.6 billion and could increase to 1.9 billion by 2020. And there are more than 1 billion children under the age of 10 that will soon follow them into adolescence. By 2020 the number of women of reproductive age in less-developed nations will grow by 24 percent. At the same time—and this is the second wave—more young women and men want to delay childbearing and to have at most two or three children.[35]

Today, 525 million women use contraception, and that number is projected to reach 742 million by 2015. While 65 percent of the world's 1 billion married women are using contraceptives, surveys among women in Rwanda, Guatemala, and other developing nations have found that between one-quarter and two-thirds are not using any form of contraception with their partners, even though they do not want any more children. Presumably as this gap between intentions and practice shrinks, demand for contraceptives will rise even faster. It is unlikely that this growth in demand can be satisfied without increased assistance to the developing countries where the growth is most dramatic.[36]

In some countries, the contraceptive shortage has already

arrived. In July 2001, Indonesia revealed that its stock of contraceptives for low-income couples would run out by the end
of the year. Few nations or agencies have developed strategies
for meeting the rising demand for contraception, and the gap
between demand and supply could simply widen over time.
Between rising numbers of young people and growing proportions wanting to plan their families, worldwide demand for
contraception is expected to grow by 40 percent between
2000 and 2015. UNFPA has estimated that global spending on
contraceptives will need to rise from $810 million annually in
2000 to $1.8 billion in 2015. The cost of making these con-
traceptives accessible through quality services will also more
than double, from $4 billion in 2000 to $9 billion in 2015.[37]

The impact of these two waves—more young people,
with higher proportions wanting to plan pregnancies—combines with a third: the soaring need for male and female condoms to prevent HIV and other sexually transmitted infections.
Mercedes' oldest daughter, Gisselle, recently reached her fif-
teenth birthday, which makes her an adult in the eyes of her
community and the Church. It also puts her in a category of
people in which HIV/AIDS is becoming a greater threat: 45 percent of the Dominican population aged 15 to 49 infected
with the virus are women.[38] (See Box 2, pages 30 and 31.)

AIDS deaths are concentrated in the prime of life, among
those who have the most to offer their societies. South Africa,
for instance, combines a 20-percent HIV infrection rate for
adults aged 15 to 49 with a fertility rate that is low for Africa,
at fewer than three children per woman. And a recent study
there indicated that death rates are higher among women in
their twenties than among those in their sixties. (See Figure 5,
page 32.) By hollowing out the core of a nation, HIV/AIDS could
cause economic and social havoc unprecedented in the modern world.[39]

The approach most likely to slow the further spread of the
infection is the one agreed to in Cairo in 1994: a holistic
effort to maximize the prospects of every human being to
enjoy sexual expression and intentional reproduction in good
health for themselves and their children. But intervention is

not likely to be fully successful in combating HIV/AIDS while prevailing attitudes of sexual and gender relations make women vulnerable to sexual predation in many societies. "Prevention strategies," says Noeleen Hayzer, executive director of the United Nations Development Fund for Women, "must be designed with full recognition of the social factors that leave most women, particularly young women and girls, unable to negotiate safer sex or to refuse unwanted sex."[40]

The Health Hazards of Being Female

Even if all of women's reproductive health needs are met—easy-to-use and affordable contraception, access to reproductive health practitioners, the choice of a safe, legal abortion—there are a variety of hazards that impair women's ability to lead healthy lives. According to the World Health Organization, "femaleness can no longer be equated with motherhood and the scope of health research needs to shift accordingly." Becoming mothers and caretakers of children, husbands, and other family members often comes at the expense of women's own health and they suffer from a variety of health problems brought on by the nature of their domestic and outside work, their living environment, and their economic situation. [41]

Consider health-care and environmental factors, for example. Worldwide, less is spent on health care for women and girls because of their lower social status and their lack of decision-making and socio-economic power. General access to health care services is also limited for many women, especially the rural and urban poor. In many countries, it is culturally unacceptable for women to travel alone to a clinic or seek care from a male health practitioner. As a result, women are conditioned to ignore their own health problems, exacerbating the duration and severity of illness. In addition, women are frequently not guaranteed privacy or medical confidentiality and are not treated with respect by health care providers.

BOX 2

The Feminization of AIDS

More than 18 million women are living with HIV/AIDS. In 1997, women accounted for 41 percent of all adult cases. That proportion had risen to nearly 50 percent by 2001 and continues to grow. Half of all new HIV infections occur among 15- to 24-year-olds, and young women are especially vulnerable.

Sub-Saharan Africa is the hardest-hit region, with 9 percent of the population infected. In several African countries, the share of the population that is infected is in the double digits. Women account for 58 percent of adult HIV/AIDS cases, and infection rates among young women are at least twice those among young men. In some parts of Kenya and Zambia, one in four teenage girls is infected compared with one in twenty-five teenage boys. Of the 2.3 percent of the population infected in the Caribbean (the world's second most-affected region), women account for 52 percent of adult cases and 55 percent of infected 15- to 24-year-olds. On some Caribbean islands, the infection rate among girls aged 15 to 19 is five times greater than among same-aged boys as a result of sex between young women and older men.

The HIV/AIDS epidemic is growing fastest in Eastern Europe. Ukraine, heavily stricken with 250,000 infected, has a rising rate of HIV transmission through sexual activity. In the Russian Federation, reports of new infections have been doubling annually since 1998. The actual number of Russians living with HIV/AIDS is estimated to be four to five times higher than the reported figure of 173,000 in 2001. Mass unemployment, economic insecurity, and disintegrating public health systems leave young people in the region especially vulnerable. Many have fallen victim to intravenous drug use and commercial sex work, which both contribute to the spread of HIV and other sexually transmitted infections (STIs). Surveys in some cities in the Russian Federation show that most sex workers are between the ages of 17 and 23 and that condom use is erratic at best.

Biological, economic, and social factors all contribute to women's vulnerability. Women have a large surface area of reproductive tissue that is exposed to their partner's secretions during intercourse, and semen infected with HIV typically contains a higher concentration of virus than a woman's sexual secretions. Young women especially are at greater risk because their reproductive organs are immature and more likely to tear during intercourse. Women also face a high risk of acquiring other STIs, which multiply ten-fold the risk of contracting HIV when left untreated.

The economic dependency of women on their sexual partners and hus-

Box 2 (continued)

bands often means they have little bargaining power when it comes to negotiating condom use. Many live in fear of being abandoned or beaten if they resist their husbands' sexual demands. In times of extreme hardship, women may rely on "sugar daddies" to support them in exchange for sex; others turn to prostitution. The stigma of infection is also a barrier to seeking care because gender-based social norms and sexual customs prevent women from learning about reproductive health. Often, sexual coercion and gender inequities are tolerated, and double standards make it acceptable for men to have multiple sexual partners.

More than 13 million children under the age of 15 are "AIDS orphans," having lost a mother or both parents to the disease. These orphans face economic and social hardships, malnutrition, and illness, and are usually taken out of school. While grandparents and other relatives may take them in, many are left to fend for themselves.

Where women participate in agricultural production, food security at the household and community level is being seriously threatened by the spread of AIDS. Communal agricultural output in Zimbabwe, for example, has been cut in half over the past five years, largely due to AIDS.

Currently, the female condom is the only safe and effective woman-controlled HIV prevention option available. It is now nominally available in over 75 countries, but unlike other reproductive health commodities there has been relatively little public sector investment in this method by governments or international donor agencies, making it costly and relatively inaccessible. A microbicide applied in the vagina could prevent infection and still allow couples to have children, but no such product currently exists. The need is compelling and efforts are under way to develop one.

Ultimately, the real key lies in improving the status of women through education, economic empowerment, open communication, and the elimination of violence and sexual coercion. But the impact of AIDS is making it increasingly difficult to implement even the most basic of strategies to halt its spread, such as providing education. Already, affected countries are losing growing numbers of teachers to AIDS. In the Central African Republic, 85 percent of teachers who died between 1996 and 1998 were HIV-positive, dying an average of 10 years before they were due to retire. Without a swift and concerted response to the epidemic, the burden of disease is likely to increase.

—Radhika Sarin, Worldwatch Institute Staff Researcher

Source: See endnote 38.

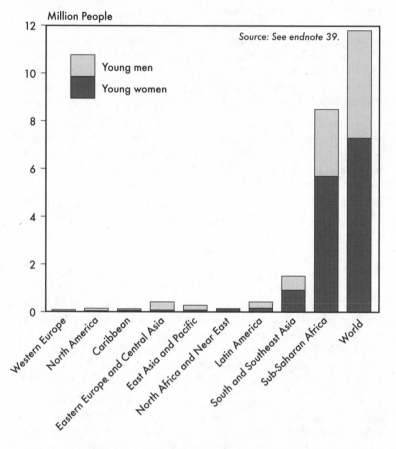

FIGURE 5

Number of HIV-Infected Women and Men Ages 15-24, December 2001

Million People

Source: See endnote 39.

Young men
Young women

Western Europe · North America · Caribbean · Eastern Europe and Central Asia · East Asia and Pacific · North Africa and Near East · Latin America · South and Southeast Asia · Sub-Saharan Africa · World

These factors prevent women from understanding the full range of options and services available to them, which can lead to unnecessary surgery and inappropriate medication to control their conditions. Women's workloads also prevent them from obtaining medical care because they simply can't afford to leave fields untended or household chores undone. [42]

By increasing their workload, environmental deterioration can affect women in different, and often more drastic, ways than men. The burden of finding clean drinking water, for instance, falls most heavily on women. (Mercedes knows she must boil or put small amounts of bleach into her drinking water to prevent illness. But many women lack the knowledge to prevent waterborne diseases, risking their health and the health of their families. A study in La Argelia, Ecuador, found that while many women boil their water for drinking, they fail to do it long enough to kill bacteria and pathogens.)[43]

Both women and men are exposed to an increasing number of environmental hazards, especially in poor rural and urban areas. Male farmers and laborers, especially in the developing world, come into contact with an array of pesticides, solvents, chemicals, and unknown toxins through their work. But because women have multiple roles—as mothers, family caretakers, farmers, and laborers—their reliance on the environment requires that they spend more time then men doing certain tasks. Mercedes' dependence on an erratic supply of water, for instance, means that she and other women in her *barrio*, not their husbands or sons, spend hours each week carrying water either from the tap near her home or from neighbors' water supplies.[44]

Indoor air pollution can be a serious threat for women. The higher concentrations of pollutants released indoors mean that they are 1,000 times more likely to reach people's lungs than pollutants released outdoors. As a result, cooking can be a high-risk activity for women, placing them in direct contact with a variety of contaminants for hours, or even days, at a time. The dangers are particularly acute among poor women in Southeast Asia, who depend upon biomass (wood, dung, and agricultural waste) or coal as fuel for preparing meals. In rural Pakistan, smoke-filled huts frequently expose women to the toxins emitted from burning wood and dung for much of the day. The effect of these factors on women's and girl's health—aggravated by cold weather, monsoons, and lack of proper ventilation—is evident in the rise of bronchitis and other respiratory diseases. Rates of asthma—which can be caused by repeated exposure to indoor pollutants, like dust and cockroach waste—in the developing world are soaring among adults, particularly women. Even in the United States, asthma death rates are nearly 20 percent higher for women than men.[45]

In addition to cooking, women produce a substantial portion of the world's food (up to 80 percent in some regions). As a result, many come into contact with a variety of pesticides, herbicides, insecticides, and fertilizers during soil preparation, planting, and harvest. Like men, women carry the pesticides on their clothing and skin, exposing children and others in the home to poisonous residue.[46]

Even when they are not involved in farming, women wash clothing soiled with chemicals or pesticides, or use containers contaminated with them to transport water and food. In Mercedes' neighborhood, old oil drums and plastic buckets that once held cleaning fluids or chemicals make convenient but highly toxic containers for water. Women also expose children directly to chemicals during pregnancy, through their breast milk, and during food preparation.

Poor sanitation—2.4 billion people lack clean water and toilets—is especially problematic for girls and women. Women's anatomy, their fear of exposing themselves in public places, and the cultural taboos and restrictions surrounding menstruation can restrict their ability to attend to biological needs. For example, women in Ethiopia who lack access to latrines become "prisoners of daylight" because they are ashamed to defecate during the day. Those who can't wait for nightfall are forced to walk long distances to find an isolated spot, exposing themselves to attacks from both men and animals.[47]

When water is scarce or when eroded and degraded soils no longer produce enough food, dietary practices can change dramatically for women and men in developing countries. Because poor women and children in many places eat last and least, such nutritional changes affect them disproportionately. Environmental degradation leads to greater expenditures of energy by women and girls because they must travel farther each day for firewood or clean water. For example, deforestation in the Sudan has quadrupled the amount of time women spend gathering wood for cooking, and the energy used to tote water from rivers and other water sources accounts for one-third of a woman's daily calorie intake, according to the WHO.

Households forced to economize on fuel because of defor-estation and poverty eat less nutritious foods, cook less often, and cook foods less thoroughly, which can lead to malnutri-tion and food-borne illness.[48]

In addition to the risks posed by health-care and envi-ronmental factors, women are often especially vulnerable to physical dangers, even in the places where they should feel the safest. For millions of girls and women, their tents, huts, and houses are places of violence and abuse by husbands, fathers, and other so-called loved ones. Along with the sounds of merengue and crowing roosters in Mercedes' *barrio*, one often hears the sound of slaps and the cries of women and children being beaten. Those are sounds heard the world over, from North American suburbs to villages in China. Violence against women, says UN Secretary General Kofi Annan "is one of the most shameful of all human rights violations." Its pervasive-ness around the world transcends economic, cultural, and religious boundaries and stands as the strongest indictment of current relations between the sexes. Abuse from an intimate partner is the most common form, and one in three women worldwide has experienced such abuse in her lifetime. In some nations the share of women ever abused ranges up to 52 percent, according to the World Health Organization. This pic-ture of abuse is a conservative one at best: shame, fear, lack of legal rights, and gender inequality keep many women from reporting their attackers. According to researchers Charlotte Watts and Cathy Zimmerman of the London School of Hygiene and Tropical Medicine, "violence against women is not only a manifestation of sex inequality, but also serves to maintain this unequal balance of power."[49] (See Table 2, page 36.)

Many men consider sex an unconditional right, and fear of reprisal can prevent girls and women from discussing con-traception or their sexual rights with partners. The United Nations reports that women in Kenya and Zimbabwe hide their birth control pills for fear that their husbands might discover that they no longer control their wives' fertility. In several African countries, most HIV-infected teenagers are female, reflecting the power of older men and the relative powerless-

TABLE 2

Examples of Violence Against Women

Neglect of Girl Children	At any one time, an estimated 60 million girls who would otherwise be expected to be alive are considered "missing" because of sex-selective abortions, infanticide, or lack of medical care and food.
Female Genital Cutting	In Ethiopia, nearly 85 percent of girls have had their genitalia cut or cut out; in Somalia, the figure is more than 95 percent. Worldwide, on any given day more than 6,000 girls are at risk of undergoing these procedures due to their ethnic or religious backgrounds.
Domestic Violence	One in three women worldwide has been abused in her lifetime and estimates (by country) of the share of women ever abused range from 16 to 52 percent.
Rape	In the United States, 1.5 million women are raped annually and 14 to 20 percent of women will be raped in their lifetimes.
Murders	In India, more than 5,000 brides are killed annually because their families are unable or unwilling to pay the dowry promised at marriage.
Honor Killings	As many as 5,000 young women worldwide died at the hands of their parents or other relatives in 2000 for "shaming" their families by having sex, socializing with boys, or becoming victims of rape.

Source: See endnote 49.

ness of girls to negotiate whether and under what conditions they have sex.[50]

Young girls married off to older men are neither emotionally nor physically prepared for their first sexual experience. And because of their age and lack of education, many girls are unable to say no or insist that their husbands use birth control, which can condition them to years of submissiveness in determining when they have sex or how many children to bear. A variety of health problems afflicts girls who start having children before their bodies are physically mature. Obstetric fistula, for example, affects more than 2 million young women in the world as a result of difficult childbirths and lack of reproductive health care. This painful and humiliating injury leaves a hole between the bladder or rectum and vagina, leading to incontinence. Stunted growth caused by malnutrition can exacerbate the problem, as can long labors. While obstetric fistula is easily correctable with minor surgery, poverty forces many of these women—some as young as 12—to live in shame because they cannot control their bladders. It can also lead to other, more serious, health problems, including fatal bladder infections.[51]

Women also experience particular dangers when war and ethnic conflict come to their communities. In Rwanda, women gave birth to between 2,000 and 5,000 *enfantes de mauvais souvenirs* (children of bad memories) as a result of rapes committed during the genocide. Estimates of the number of women raped in Croatia and Bosnia-Herzegovina during the late 1990s range from 14,000 to 50,000. Women refugees face multiple dangers because of their sex, including lack of reproductive health care services and sexual violence and coercion. In West African refugee camps, for instance, there are allegations that women have been forced to trade sex for food.[52]

It is no surprise that in societies where women are treated as second-class citizens, they are much more likely than men to take their own lives. Females in some parts of Turkey, Afghanistan, and Iran, for example, account for as much as 80 percent of all suicides, and nearly 500 women per day commit suicide in China. In these cases, the link to population change is complex but significant. Societies that treat women as property or otherwise oppress them are unlikely to support the conditions needed for planned families or the delay of pregnancy and childbirth. Ending this violence will be first and foremost its own reward. The supplemental benefit for positive demographic change comes from the simple fact that women whose individual and social autonomy is denied can scarcely be free to decide for themselves when and with whom to become parents.[53]

Population Politics

After the Earth Summit, the Cairo (ICPD) conference, and the Beijing conference on women, the community of nations knows why and how improving women's lives and opportunities is a fundamental part of reducing population growth. And this work is moving forward. The global fertility rate has fallen almost by half in just 40 years. Yet the promise of reproductive health for all and equality for women remains unfulfilled. As a result, so does the vision of a world moving swiftly toward a population peak based on intended childbearing.[54]

No one contests the need to reduce unwanted fertility. This was a central message of Cairo, and the elimination of unmet need for family planning was a clear benchmark adopted at the conference's 5th year UN General Assembly Special Session review in 1999. But reducing "wanted fertility" by providing more opportunities for women was a central message, too, says Margaret Greene of Population Action International. Participants made it clear that the circumstances that encourage women to marry young and have many children are fundamentally linked to their relatively low status in society. Parents and girls need to know that there are options in addition to or outside of marriage and motherhood.[55]

At the Cairo conference, governments agreed to spend $18.5 billion by 2005 to achieve universal access to basic reproductive health services by 2015. This was to include $15.2 billion for family planning services, maternal health, and safe delivery, and $1.3 billion for prevention of HIV/AIDS and other sexually transmitted diseases. Since Cairo, the emerging deadliness of the HIV/AIDS pandemic has framed it almost as a separate health issue in international dialogue, with agreement that much more will need to be spent than the ICPD envisioned. But so far there is no consensus on just how much money will be needed in the effort to contain HIV/AIDS, what it will buy, and where it will come from.[56]

Of the original Cairo sum for family planning and other

reproductive health needs, wealthy nations pledged to cover one-third and the developing world agreed to pay the rest. In 2000, the most recent year with comprehensive data, wealthy nations contributed less than 46 percent of their Cairo commitment. By contrast, developing nations have been spending close to 73 percent of their commitment levels. (This proportion is somewhat distorted, however, by high spending in China, India, and Indonesia, with much lower spending in sub-Saharan Africa.)[57]

The U.S. contribution to Cairo spending levels has been the most disappointing. The nation with the world's largest economy should be spending $1.9 billion annually on family planning and related health programs in developing countries according to calculations by Population Action International. The current U.S. contribution, however, is $500 million for reproductive health programs (appropriated for fiscal year 2001), including $450 million for family planning and ancillary services and $50 million specifically for maternal health. Abortion-related restrictions—the "global gag rule" reinstated by the Bush administration—complicate the allocation of these funds. The gag rule, also known as the Mexico City Policy, prohibits U.S. funding to international organizations that advise their patients about terminating pregnancies. And the U.S.'s decision to eliminate $34 million dollars in funding to the UN Population Fund (UNFPA) could lead, according to UNFPA spokesperson Stirling Scruggs, to 2 million unwanted pregnancies, 800,000 abortions, almost 5,000 maternal deaths, and 77,000 infant and child deaths.[58]

Consistent with greater attention to the HIV/AIDS pandemic, the U.S. government appropriated $320 million in 2001 to combat the disease, but so far it is unclear how the money will be spent and whether it will be integrated with any other aspects of reproductive health or with efforts to promote needed changes in relations between women and men. Although an additional $500 million was proposed by the Bush administration in June 2002 for prevention, it is mostly targeted for drugs that will prevent mother-to-child transmission. This focus on protecting infants, while important, ignores the millions of women and men who contract the disease through sex or other means.[59]

Historically, the world's major religions have erected some of the most formidable barriers to increased availability of family planning services and reproductive health care in general. Some religious leaders continue to preach abstinence as the only effective and moral means of controlling births. Nonetheless, many nations have made great progress in widening access to family planning and reproductive health care and improving the status of women.[60]

Many religious leaders believe that there is no inherent conflict between family planning and religion, and that in fact lack of reproductive health services represents a grave social injustice. In Iran, Islamic clerics have even issued *fatwas* (religious edicts) approving family planning methods, from oral contraceptives and condoms to sterilization. In Iran, Shi'ism has demonstrated an openness to change, providing a useful example to other nations—especially in the Middle East— where religion and government policy are intertwined. The Qur'an is interpreted in a way that allows people to live "moral" lives without ignoring the social, economic, and population realities of the modern world. This approval, along with the integration of family planning services with primary health care, the provision of free contraceptives, and the strengthening of men's role in reproductive health, resulted in the total fertility rate in Iran dropping from 5.6 children in 1985 to 3 children in 1996 to replacement fertility of just 2 children per woman in 2002—among the most precipitous declines in family size in the modern demographic transition.[61] (See Box 3, page 42 and Figure 6, page 43.)

Where religion continues to hamper efforts to give people greater control over their reproductive lives, the world's religious leaders may need to challenge official doctrine. Bishop Kevin Dowling did just that (and risked his career) when he introduced a proposal at the Southern African Catholic Bishops conference in 2001 in support of condom use as part of the wider effort to stop the spread of HIV in his region, which has the highest HIV infection rate in the world. Although the proposal was rejected and the Church remains aggressively opposed to condom use, Bishop Dowling's efforts give some sense of the leadership that will be needed if religious institutions are to work with others in the fight against HIV/AIDS and other public health problems related to reproduction.[62]

There is often a gap between the opinions of church leaders and church members on reproductive issues. For example, it emerged during the UN Special Session on Children in May of 2002 that most predominantly Catholic nations did not support the Vatican's stance on reproductive health issues. Many Latin American countries, as well as 99-percent-Catholic Spain, called for comprehensive reproductive health services and "high quality sexual education" for children.[63]

This gap mirrors a wider chasm between elected officials and their civic constituencies. According to a recent Gallup poll, for example, over 75 percent of Mexicans believe in a woman's right to choose abortion. Yet Mexico's politicians oppose reforms allowing women and couples greater access to safe abortion procedures. Conservative U.S. politicians, too, would like to see *Roe v. Wade*, the 1973 Supreme Court decision legalizing abortion in the United States, overturned. And they continue to stymie efforts to fund international family planning programs, even though opinion polls show that the vast majority of Americans support both a woman's right to control her own fertility and U.S. efforts in this area overseas.[64]

A misconception spread by some political and religious organizations clouds this discussion and muzzles debate: the idea that providing choices about pregnancy and childbearing is synonymous with the promotion of abortion. Because of groundless allegations that the UNFPA endorses forced sterilizations and abortions in foreign nations, the Bush administration has eliminated U.S. funding to the UN for reproductive health. Although lawmakers and President Bush agreed to appropriate $34 million in funding to UNFPA last year, anti-choice advocates lobbied for a freeze on spending for health-related services for women in all nations. Ironically, demographic research confirms what logic tells us: wider provision of good family planning services reduces the numbers

BOX 3
Youth and Reproductive Health

Almost 40 percent of Iran's 67 million people are between the ages of 10 and 24 years. This disproportionately youthful population and the population boom of the 1980's forced Iranian leaders to focus on education and the family planning needs of youth and married couples. The result has been dramatic. Over the past two decades total fertility not only fell (see Figure 6), but literacy rates for young women almost doubled, from 48 to 92 percent. However, discussion of youth sexual and reproductive health matters still makes many policy makers uncomfortable. Most education about family planning and reproductive health is focused on engaged couples and the government heavily censors books and pamphlets about reproduction in schools.

The Netherlands, on the other hand, has instituted policies that encourage openness concerning the sexual and reproductive needs of adolescents, regardless of whether they are engaged or married. Most secondary schools include sexuality education in their curricula, and mass media campaigns about preventing HIV/AIDS and other sexually transmitted infections encourage youth and their parents to talk about sex, contraception, and reproductive health. The Catholic Church in the Netherlands expressed hostility toward premarital sex and family planning in the 1970s, but today Dutch Church leaders have realized that modern lifestyles and family values can go hand in hand and that youth need support to make healthy sexual and reproductive decisions. The Netherlands commitment to emphasizing "quality, tolerance, and respect at the center of social and political life" has led to one of the lowest total fertility rates in the world—just 1.7 births per woman—and more importantly, generations of young people who feel supported and empowered to make their own decisions about sexuality.

Source: See endnote 61.

of abortions that would otherwise occur. For example, when researchers looked at two similar areas of rural Bangladesh, one with good family planning services and the other without, they found that abortion rates had increased over the past two decades in the one with poor family planning services but had held steady at low rates in the area with good services.[65]

Just as important as spending levels are the political atti-

FIGURE 6

Estimated Total Fertility Rate in Iran, 1950-2002

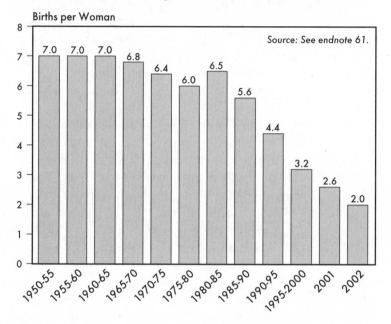

Births per Woman

Source: See endnote 61.

tudes that shape and expand population policies and reproductive health programs around the world. In the spirit of
Cairo, governments in Africa, Asia, and Latin America are
rethinking population policies and programs and looking to
the Programme of Action for guidance on new directions
related to overall health and development. Progress is uneven.
On the one hand, the governor of the Indian state of Andhra
Pradesh has publicly urged the parents of large families to
immediately go for state-sponsored sterilizations, and China's
central government resists the key principle of reproductive freedom of choice by continuing to advocate that most Chinese
couples limit their families to a single child, although the
one-child rule is no longer a part of formal policy. On the other
hand, the government has at least acknowledged the importance of the principles agreed to at Cairo and is expanding the
voluntary choice program started with UNFPA support in 32

counties to another 800 counties. And India's federal government is abandoning its decades-long history of targets and quotas for family planning and its reliance on sterilization rather than the contraceptives that are more appropriate for tens of millions of couples. The overall movement among national governments in developing countries is clearly away from bureaucratically imposed population control and toward supporting the choices of couples and individuals to have children, when desired, in good health.[66]

With the emergence of strong women's NGOs in the decade since Cairo, full political participation by women in national politics may become the last and most important frontier in achieving the gender equity needed for truly sustainable societies. Higher rates of illiteracy, poverty, and other social and economic handicaps conspire against political participation by women, and women remain underrepresented at all levels of government in almost all countries. (See Figure 2, page 20.) There has been some progress, but women's share of seats in lower chambers of parliaments grew only from 3 percent in 1945 to 14 percent in 2001. Typically, women leaders are steered into less powerful sectors of government, such as health and education, with much smaller numbers of women holding key economic and executive positions. Although sexual and reproductive rights command little attention in debates over democracy, once gained they allow women to achieve self-determination and are thus intimately linked to the meaning of modern citizenship.[67]

Evidence from Sweden, South Africa, India, and other nations shows that when more women hold political office, issues important to women and their families rise in priority and are acted on by those in power. Over the past decade, the Swedish government—where women currently hold almost 43 percent of the seats in Parliament and 82 percent of the cabinet ministries—has passed expansive equal opportunity and child care leave acts. And in South Africa, which established a quota for women candidates to parliament in 2000, women hold 119 of the 399 seats in the National Assembly and 8 of the 29 cabinet positions. These female politicians have played a key role in lobbying for the Choice of Termination of Pregnancy Act and the Domestic Violence Act and in establishing governmental institutions that promote gender equality.[68]

Gender Equity and Resource Use

The number of people on Earth combines with levels of consumption, dominant technologies, and distribution of income to determine humanity's use of resources. Gender inequity can be a potent force within the human factor of this equation. For the most part, men are responsible for deciding how the world's natural resources are used through mining, grazing of livestock, and logging. Development agencies still tend to offer technical and agricultural assistance exclusively to men even in areas where women are the ones toting the fuelwood and water and tilling the soil.

In the past decade, the international development community has intensified its focus on women's stewardship of natural resources. "Since rights to natural resources are so heavily biased against women," reasons Agnes Quisumbing of the International Food Policy Research Institute, "equalizing these rights will lead to more efficient and equitable resource use." When government officials or community leaders fail to recognize the different ways women use natural resources—growing vegetables for family consumption in the spaces between male-managed cash crops, for example—the resources are easily destroyed. For example, to protect fragile mangroves in El Salvador, community officials placed restrictions on fishing and collecting fuel wood. The community's women, who depended on both the wood and the fish from the estuaries to feed their families, were not consulted—but they were most affected by the ban because performing their role as caretakers became a criminal act. Such inefficiencies are no longer tolerable in view of the increasing stresses on croplands and other resources imposed by rising populations.[69]

But women are not only victims of environmental degra-

dation; they are activists as well, and many have acted to protect natural resources by mobilizing their communities against
environmental and health hazards. Women in India, for
instance, are resisting large-scale agricultural methods that
require heavy inputs of chemicals by promoting sustainable
agriculture in rural communities. In the Ogoni region of Nigeria, women have come together to fight the toll that oil pollution—fires, oil waste dumping, and pipe explosions—has
taken on the health of their families and the environment.
Their demands have included protection of women environmental activists and compensation for health damages from
the oil industry. In the region of Louisiana known as "Cancer
Alley," African-American women are educating one another and
their communities about the connections linking industry, environment, and human health.[70]

When women gain rights to land or other resources and
the ability to protect and conserve them, they also gain power
that reaches well beyond forests or watersheds. By com-
manding a concrete resource, notes Indian economist Bina
Agarwal, women can improve their self-sufficiency, reduce
their dependence on men, and strengthen their bargaining posi-
tion within their marriages, including their ability to negotiate contraceptive use with their husbands. These redefined
relationships produce benefits—healthier families, better education of girls and boys, and a cleaner environment—that
ripple out into the broader community.[71]

The strong role women are often able to play in environmental stewardship and activism points to the value of integrating reproductive health and family planning components
into conservation programs. In the 1970s, northern NGOs
concerned with improving rural environments and reducing
poverty in the Philippines and Nepal began to offer improved
access to family planning services. As interest in family planning expanded, other organizations partnered with national
and regional family planning organizations to respond to
women's requests for help with avoiding pregnancy. More
recently, in Madagascar's Spiny Forest Ecoregion—home to the
greatest concentration of baobab trees in the world—the World

Wildlife Fund (WWF) produced maps showing that where female literacy levels were the lowest, both population growth rates and deforestation were the highest. Based on this, WWF fieldworkers and local stakeholders formed a partnership with a Malagasy regional public health organization to deliver literacy programs, reproductive health information, and family planning services to communities with both the highest population growth and the greatest levels of biodiversity.[72]

Similarly, Conservation International (CI) is helping to improve access to reproductive health care near biologically rich areas in the Philippines and Guatemala. And in the southern Mexican state of Chiapas, in communities around one of the country's last primary forests, a CI project links agricultural training, improved access to reproductive health care, and micro-credit loans for women.[73]

The Jane Goodall Institute is working to improve women's status and the environment in the villages surrounding Gombe National Park in Tanzania. There, they are combining conservation education, training in sustainable agriculture, and the establishment of woodlots that reduce the time women spend gathering wood with preventive health care, family planning, and information about sexually transmitted diseases, including HIV/AIDS. The result is that women are becoming more effective household and resource managers as well as entrepeneurs because they have the access and means to start their own small, environmentally sustainable businesses.[74]

These initiatives demonstrate that incorporating improved access to contraception and other reproductive health services can increase women's participation in natural resource conservation or functional literacy programs and vice versa. As the connections between conservation and population projects become clearer, the environmental community and environment ministers can become an important new constituency for reproductive health and women's rights. Investments to slow the rate of population growth will significantly reinforce efforts to address many environmental challenges, and considerably lower the price of such efforts.[75]

A New Vision

At the Rio Earth Summit in 1992, women came together as never before and presented their vision of a world in which all women are educated, free from violence, and able to make their own reproductive choices. As a result of this mobilization, the Rio Declaration and Agenda 21 call for women's full participation in sustainable development and improvement in their status at all levels of society.

The work that began at the Earth Summit did not end there. Because of the efforts made in Rio by women's NGOs, women's health and human rights have made their way onto the international agenda. Rio's Agenda 21 set the stage for the ICPD in Cairo in 1994. There, the Cairo Programme of Action reaffirmed women's rights and their equal participation in all spheres of society as a prerequisite for better human development.

Despite such progress and the evidence of its benefits, gender myopia continues to cloud the vision needed by development agencies, international lenders, and governments. From agriculture to trade liberalization and health care reforms, policy decisions affect women in quite distinct ways. If their specific concerns are not made part of the policy process, the results can be disastrous. But seeing things through a gender lens requires a very different course for development—one that includes women and other marginalized groups—in planning and decisionmaking. Rachel Kyte, a senior specialist at the International Finance Corporation, argues that even now, a full decade after Rio, "it's very difficult to talk about the rights of women when the development industry remains truly patriarchal." Gender, by this view, is still not a central issue in development, perhaps in part because it so fundamentally challenges men's power.[76]

It is unlikely that Mercedes knows what happened at the Earth Summit, the ICPD, or this year's World Summit on Sustainable Development in Johannesburg, South Africa. Mercedes and millions of women like her are unaware of international policies related to gender and population, not out of apathy or lack of intelligence, but simply because the promises made at such events have yet to make a difference in their daily lives. Until the commitments made at these conferences are upheld by governments, these women will see little improvement in their relations to men, their access to reproductive and general health care, their control over natural resources, or their ability to participate fully in politics.

"Ultimately the changes needed to make women equal partners in development," wrote Jodi Jacobson in 1992 shortly after Rio, "are the same as those required to sustain life itself." Improving women's lives and the health of children, families, and the environment requires asking what both women and men want and need, not simply limiting their reproductive capacity. Universal access to contraceptives and fulfillment of the commitments made in Cairo in 1994 are critical, but other steps are needed as well.[77]

Making sure that girls and young women are in school can sometimes be even more effective than improved sanitation, employment, or a higher income in helping children survive. The nations in sub-Saharan Africa with the highest levels of female schooling—Botswana, Kenya, and Zimbabwe—are also the nations with the lowest levels of child mortality and fertility, despite higher levels of poverty than some of their neighbors. A study from the International Food Policy Research Institute found that improvements in women's education were responsible for 43 percent of the reduction in child malnutrition in the developing world in the last 25 years.[78] (See Figure 7 on page 50.)

These benefits across generations appear to result from women's tendency to devote higher proportions of their personal income than men do to the needs of their children. A study in Brazil found that additional income in the hands of mothers was 20 times more likely to improve child survival than the same income earned by fathers. In general, as David Dollar and Roberta Gatti of the World Bank state, "Societies that have a preference for not investing in girls pay a price in terms of slower growth and reduced income." In countries

---

FIGURE 7

Shares of Reduction in Child Malnutrition Attributed to Underlying Variables, 1970-95

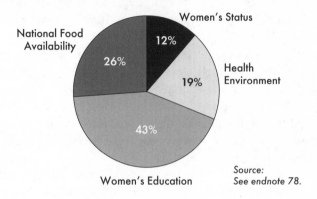

National Food Availability 26%

Women's Status 12%

Health Environment 19%

Women's Education 43%

Source: See endnote 78.

where less than three-fourths as many females as males are enrolled in primary and secondary school, for example, per capita income is roughly one-fourth lower than in other countries. There can be little doubt that increases in income that have their roots in the education of girls and women also help build societies in which women on average have fewer children and give birth later in their lives.[79]

Correcting gender myopia means creating a new vision for the world, one that includes women as decisionmakers and active participants. There are encouraging signs along this front. Today, more NGOs than ever consist of women advocating for women's rights, empowerment, and health. The gap between the numbers of boys and girls in schools is beginning to close. Women leaders are making their presence known in city councils, state governments, and international institutions.[80]

For the vision of Cairo to be completely realized, however, the ICPD Programme of Action needs to be fully funded to provide reproductive health services, including contraception, maternal care, and sexually transmitted disease prevention, for all who seek them. Ideally, more generous spending than the Cairo conference foresaw would be forthcoming to improve and fully integrate the entire range of reproductive health services, including HIV/AIDS prevention and basic treatment as well as access to safe abortion. At a minimum, honoring the Cairo spending goal could well be more effective than any other single effort in improving the lives of women and bringing population growth to an early peak based on intentional and healthy childbearing.

As the growing concerns about population aging and decline in some countries suggest, it is increasingly possible that world population growth will end within the next 50 years. We should encourage this historic process, resisting the urge expressed in some countries to roll back population aging by stoking continued population growth. We can work, as well, to make sure that the end to that growth is driven by intended reductions in births, not by increases in deaths from HIV/AIDS and other diseases.

The relationship between progress toward gender equity and progress in controlling population has become all but undeniable. To build on this understanding requires that nations take the following steps:

• **Commit to meet or exceed the goals set at Cairo and remove barriers to comprehensive and reproductive health care at the national level.** At Cairo, governments agreed to spend $17 billion a year (in 1993 dollars) by 2000 to achieve universal access to basic reproductive health services for all by 2015. To date, the world's poorest nations are spending close to three-fourths of their committed levels. Spending levels in wealthy nations have yet to reach even half of their Cairo commitment.[81]

• **Persuade the United States to remove the barriers to funding for international family planning.** President Bush should immediately rescind the global gag rule, which prohibits U.S. funding to international agencies that even talk about abortion with their clients. And the administration should deliver on its promise of $34 million in funding for the United Nations Population Fund and not push governments to promote abstinence-only programs to prevent unwanted pregnancies.[82]

• **Increase the number of women holding public office.** The Women's Environment and Development Organization and other groups have called for 50/50 representation at all levels, from local village councils to the highest offices in national parliaments.[83]

• **Remove obstacles that prevent girls from attending school.** Study after study shows that girls with more education not only have fewer and healthier babies, but enjoy better health themselves. [84]

• **Educate men and boys about the importance of gender equity and shared responsibility.** Stereotypes and cultural expectations about masculinity prevent many men from taking responsibility for reproductive health and child care. Some feel threatened by women's independence and express their manhood through violence or withholding money from their families. These fears and stereotypes can be changed. In Nicaragua, workshops for unlearning *machismo* and improving communication skills have led to less domestic violence. And in Mali, male volunteers have been trained to provide information about reproductive health and family planning and distribute contraceptives.[85]

• **Increase youth awareness about reproductive health issues, including HIV/AIDS and other sexually transmitted diseases.** In places like Uganda and Senegal, government commitment to AIDS education at both the national and village level has helped bring the epidemic in those nations under control. In Mexico, peer counseling programs allow young people to talk to and be educated by their peers about sexual health and to communicate more openly with their elders about sexuality and family planning.[86]

• **Enact and enforce strong laws that protect women from violence.** Many national laws trap women in violent relationships or make it impossible to prosecute men for beatings, rape, and other forms of abuse. Some countries—Mexico and the Philippines, for instance—have revised their rape laws, making the act a "crime against one's freedom." In Belize and Malaysia, laws and penal codes have been reformed to criminalize domestic violence.[87]

Such policy changes, if carried out thoroughly and in good faith, could transform the lives of hundreds of millions of people, and not only women; changing the social and economic conditions that discriminate against Mercedes, Gisselle, and Gina will improve Jonathon's life as well. And history will note that world population growth ended not because governments commanded it, but because the free decisions of women and men made that end inevitable. The population peak will arrive as one momentous ripple from an equally momentous drop of a stone in a pond—the stone by which women at last gain their full rights, choices, and standing as equal members of the human family.

Notes

1.   Oficina Nacional de Estadistica de la Republica Dominicana, Licitacion VIII Censo Nacional, www.one.gov.do/, viewed 30 May 2002; *World Gazetteer Population Statistics*, <www.world-gazetteer.com/c/c_do.htm>, viewed 31 May 2002.

2.   Ibid.

3.   Population Reference Bureau, *Women of Our World 2002*, wall chart (Washington, DC: PRB, 2002).

4.   United Nations, *World Population Prospects: The 2000 Revision* (New York: 2001).

5.   Nafis Sadik, "Working Towards Gender Equality in Marriage," *Innocenti Digest*, March 2001, p. 18.

6.   United Nations, *Report of the International Conference on Population and Development, Cairo, 5–13 September 1994*, Programme of Action of the International Conference on Population and Development, Annex to the Report (New York: 18 October 1994).

7.   Perdita Huston, *Families As We Are: Conversations From Around the World* (New York: The Feminist Press at the University of New York, 2001), p. 334.

8.   John Cleland, "Equity, Security, and Fertility: A Reaction to Thomas, *Population Studies*, July 1993, p. 351.

9.   Figure and historical estimates from Robert Engelman, Population Action International, based on various written works by historians and demographers; for historical estimates, see also see U.S. Bureau of Census, "Historical Estimates of World Population," <www.census.gov/ipc/www/worldhis.html>; United Nations, op. cit. note 4); New York City population from U.S. Census Bureau 2000 census, at <www.ci.nyc.ny.us/html/dcp/html/pop2000.html>, viewed 18 October 2001.

10.   Population would have topped 8 billion from Patrick Heuveline, "The Global Impact of Mortality and Fertility Transitions, 1950–2000," *Population and Development Review*, December 1999, pp. 681–702; data on fertility and population change from United Nations, op. cit. note 4); "UN Study: Population Boom a Bust," *New York Times*, 12 March 2002; Hans Greimel, "Work Less, Have More Babies Government Says in Report on Nation's Lifestyle," Associated Press wire story, 26 March 2002; Peter G. Peterson, "Gray Dawn: The Global Aging Crisis," *Foreign Affairs*, January/February 1999, pp. 42–55; Phillip J. Longman, "The Global Aging Crisis," *U.S. News & World Report*, 1 March 1999, pp. 30–39; data on fertility and population change from United Nations, op. cit. note 4.

11. Emma Daly, "UN Says Elderly Will Soon Outnumber Young for First Time," *New York Times*, 9 April 2002, p. 6; United Nations Department of Economic and Social Affairs Population Division, *World Population Monitoring 2000: Population, Gender, and Development* (New York: United Nations, 2001), p. 127; two to five times figure from United Nations Department of Economic and Social Affairs, *Aging 1950-2050* (New York: United Nations, 2001), pp. xxix and 70; Second World Assembly on Aging Joint Statement by Thoraya Obaid, Executive Director, UN Population Fund, and Mark Malloch-Brown, Administrator, UN Development Programme, Madrid, 8-12 April 2002, <www.unfpa.org/about/ed/2002/ageing_joint.htm>, viewed 12 April 2002; United Nations, *The World's Women 2000: Trends and Statistics* (New York: United Nations, 2000), p. 75; United Nations Department of Economic and Social Affairs Population Division, "World Population Aging 1950-2050 (New York: United Nations, 2001), p. 74; osteoporosis from International Osteoporosis Foundation, "The Facts About Osteoporosis and Its Impact," <www.osteofound.org/press_centre/fact_sheet.html>, viewed 30 May 2002.

12.   United Nations, op. cit. note 4; Population Reference Bureau, *World Population Data Sheet 2002*, wall chart (Washington, DC: 2002).

13.   185 million figure from preliminary estimates by the United Nations Population Division, Coordination Meeting on International Migration, 11-12 July 2002; International Organization for Migration (IOM) and United Nations, *World Migration Report 2000* (New York: 2000), p. 3; global migration data from United Nations, *International Migration and Development: The Concise Report* (New York: 1997); National Intelligence Council, *Growing Global Migration and Its Implications for the United States* (Washington, DC: 2001). Box 1: Beth Gardiner, "Trucker Found Guilty in the Suffocation Deaths of 58 Immigrants," Associated Press wire story, 5 April 2001; "U.S. Promises Action after Mexican Migrants' Deaths," *Arizona Republic*, 24 May 2001; James Sterngold, "Devastating Picture of Immigrants Dead in the Arizona Desert," *New York Times*, 24 May 2001; Thomas Homer-Dixon, *Environment, Scarcity, and Violence* (Princeton, NJ: Princeton University Press, 1999), p. 110; Women migrants from IOM and UN, op. cit. this note; trafficking from UN Population Fund (UNFPA), *The State of World Population 2000* (New York: 2000), p. 29; remittances from IOM and UN, op. cit. this note; Population Reference Bureau, *Women, Men, and Environmental Change: The Gender Dimensions of Environmental Policies and Programs* (Washington, DC: PRB, 2002), p. 2.

14.   Estimate of developing-country contraceptive prevalence in the late 1960s from J. Khanna, P.F.A. Van Look and P.D. Griffin, *Reproductive Health: Key to a Brighter Future*, World Health Organization Biennial Report 1990–1991 (Geneva: World Health Organization, 1992), pp. 5, 6; modern contraceptive prevalence from Population Reference Bureau, *2001 World Population Data Sheet*, wall chart (Washington, DC: June 2001).

15.   Estimate of unmet need from John A. Ross and William L. Winfrey, "Unmet Need in the Developing World and the Former USSR: An Updated Estimate," unpublished manuscript, received 1 November 2001; 350 million from UN Population Fund, *The State of World Population 1999* (New York: 1999), p. 2.

16. Nancy E. Riley, "Gender, Power, and Population Change," *Population Bulletin*, May 1997; effects of education in high-fertility countries from United Nations, Population Division, *Women's Education and Fertility Behaviour: Recent Evidence from the Demographic and Health Surveys* (New York: 1995), p. 29.

17. Barbara Mensch, Judith Bruce, and Margaret Greene, *The Uncharted Passage: Girls' Adolescence in the Developing World* (New York: Population Council, 1998), p. 29.

18. United Nations, *The World's Women 2000*, op.cit. note 11, p. 85; UN Educational, Cultural, and Scientific Organization (UNESCO) Institute for Statistics, Assessment of February 2002, <www.uis.unesco.org/en/stats/statistics/UIS Lit_Regional_2002.xls>; UNESCO, Statistical Yearbook 1999 Database, <www.unescostat.unesco.org/en/stats/stats0.htm>, viewed 29 July 2002.

19. United Nations, *The World's Women 2000*, op. cit. note 11, pp. 86 and 132; Johnson quote from Alan Cowell, "French Politics Finds Little Room for Women," *New York Times*, 7 June 2002, p. 3. Table 1: education from United Nations, op. cit. note 11, pp. 87, 91, and from UN Population Fund (UNFPA), *The State of World Population 2001* (New York: 2001), p. 41; women-headed households' vulnerability from International Fund for Agricultural Development, *Rural Poverty Report 2001* (New York: Oxford University Press, 2001), pp. 28–29; Allen Dupree and Wendell Primus, *Declining Share of Children Lived With Single Mothers in the Late 1990s: Substantial Differences by Race and Income* (Washington, DC: Center on Budget and Policy Priorities, 2001); women's earnings from United Nations, op. cit. this note; one-third from UNFPA, op. cit. this note, p. 38; 500 largest corporations from United Nations, op. cit. this note, p. 130; International Monetary Fund from UNIFEM, *Progress of the World's Women 2000* (New York: United Nations Development Fund for Women, 2000), p. 32; International Women's Democracy Center, "Women's Political Participation," fact sheet, at <www.iwdc.org/factsheets.htm>, viewed 23 July 2001; Women's Environment and Development Organization (WEDO), "Fact Sheet 3: Women in Government: Get the Balance Right," at <www.wedo.org/fact_sheet_3.htm>, viewed 17 October 2001; civic freedom from David Dollar and Roberta Gatti, *Gender Inequality, Income, and Growth: Are Good Times Good for Women?* (Washington, DC: World Bank Development Research Group, 1999), pp. 5, 6. Figure 2: Nada Chaya, et al., *A World of Difference: Sexual and Reproductive Health and Risks (PAI Report Card 2001)* , wall chart and report (Washington, DC: Population Action International, 2001). Women's work hours from World Bank, *Engendering Development: Through Gender Equality in Rights, Resources, and Voice* (New York: Oxford University Press, 2001), pp. 152–54; one-third share from UNFPA, op. cit. note 13, p. 38; two-thirds to three-fourths from United Nations, op. cit. note 11, pp. 131-132. Figure 3: ibid., Updated Table 5.G available online at <unstats.un.org/unsd/demo graphic/ww2000/table5g.htm>, viewed July 30, 2002.

20. Robert Lalasz, "Does Population Matter? New Research on Population Change and Economic Development," *PECS News: A Population, Environmental Change, and Security Newsletter,* The Woodrow Wilson Center, Spring 2002, p. 3. Canlas quoted in Doris C. Dumlao, "Gov't To Adopt 'Population Management Plan,' Says NEDA," *Philippine Daily Inquirer,* 27 June 2001.

21. David E. Bloom and Jeffrey G. Williamson, "Demographic Transitions and Economic Miracles in Emerging Asia," *World Bank Economic Review,* September 1998, pp. 419–455.

22. Lester Brown, Gary Gardner, and Brian Halweil, *Beyond Malthus* (New York: W.W. Norton & Company, 1999); sub-Saharan Africa from ibid., pp. 91–92.

23. United Nations, Population Division, Department of Economic and Social Affairs, *World Urbanization Prospects, The 1999 Revision* (New York: 1999); Martin Brockerhoff and Ellen Brennan, *The Poverty of Cities in the Developing World,* Policy Research Division Working Paper No. 96 (New York: Population Council, 1997), p. 5; maternal mortality in Caribbean, Population Reference Bureau, op. cit. note 3.

24. Thoraya Obaid, Executive Director, UN Population Fund, discussion with Brian Halweil, Curtis Runyan, and Danielle Nierenberg, April 2002; Christian G. Mesquida and Neil I. Wiener, "Male Age Composition and the Severity of Conflicts," *Politics in the Life Sciences,* September 1999, pp. 181–89; for population and environmental scarcity connections to conflict generally, see Thomas Homer-Dixon and Valerie Percival, *Environmental Scarcity and Violent Conflict: Briefing Book* (Washington, DC: American Association for the Advancement of Science/University of Toronto, 1996).

25. The Programme of Action of the International Conference on Population and Development, <www.undp.org/popin/icpd/conference/offeng/poa.html>, viewed 23 July 2001.

26. Michelle Andrews, "Birth Control Is Changing," *New York Times,* 21 April 2002, p. 8.

27. Jane Hughes and Anne P. McCauley, "Improving the Fit: Adolescents' Needs and Future Programs for Sexual and Reproductive Health in Developing Countries," *Studies in Family Planning,* June 1998, pp. 233–45; International NGO Youth Consultation on Population and Development, "Cairo Youth Declaration," 1994, <youth.unesco.or.kr/youth/english/resources>, viewed on 18 September 2001.

28. William Orme, "UN Forum on Children Takes Up Abortion; Controversy: Delegates Argue About Whether the Phrase 'Reproductive Health Services' Should Be Included in Conference Documents," 9 May 2002, *Los Angeles Times,* p. A3; Tom Teepen, "Bush Wins at UN, While World's Children Lose," *Dayton Daily News,* 16 May 2002; "U.S. Spends 27 Million Dollars Promoting Abstinence Before Marriage," Agence France Press wire story, 2 July 2002.

29. Research on the impacts of information and guidance from Douglas Kirby, *Emerging Answers: Research Findings on Programs to Reduce Teen Pregnancy* (Washington, DC: National Campaign To Prevent Teen Pregnancy, 2001), and from Hughes and McCauley, op. cit. note 32; UN Population Fund, "Supporting the Next Generation of Parents and Leaders," <www.unfpa.org/adolescents/index.htm>, viewed 12 October 2001.

30. Rodolfo A. Bulatao, *The Value of Family Planning Programs in Developing Countries* (Washington, DC: Rand, 1998), p. 24; Hantamalala Rafalimanana and Charles F. Westoff, "Potential Effects on Fertility and Child Health and Survival of Birth-spacing Preferences in Sub-Saharan Africa," *Studies in Family Planning*, June 2000, p. 99; Figure 4 based on Nada Chaya et al., *A World of Difference: Sexual and Reproductive Health & Risks* (PAI Report Card 2001), wall chart and report (Washington, DC: Population Action International, 2001).

31. Robert Engelman, *Plan and Conserve: A Source Book on Linking Population and Environmental Services in Communities* (Washington, DC: Population Action International, 1998), pp. 22, 34–35, 42; impact of the pill on American women's education from Claudia Golden and Lawrence F. Katz, "On the Pill: Changing the Course of Women's Education," *The Milken Institute Review*, Second Quarter 2001, pp. 12–21.

32. Population Action International, "How Family Planning Protects the Health of Women and Children," fact sheet no. 2 in second series (Washington, DC: April 2001); Anne Tinker and Elizabeth Ransom, *Healthy Mothers and Healthy Newborns: The Vital Link, Policy Perspectives on Newborn Health*, <www.prb.org/pdf/HealthyMothers_Eng.pdf>, p. 1, viewed 7 June 2002; UN Children's Fund, "State of the World's Mothers," <www.savethechildren.org/mothers/pdf/factsheet.pdf>, p. 2, viewed 7 June 2002.

33. Role of family planning movement in fertility decline from John Bongaarts, W. Parker Mauldin, and James F. Phillips, "The Demographic Impact of Family Planning Programs," *Studies in Family Planning*, November/December 1990; Bulatao, op. cit. note 30, p. 24.

34. UN Population Fund, op. cit. note 13, p. 23.

35. United Nations Population Division, *World Population Prospects: The 2000 Revision, Vol. II, Sex and Age Distribution of the World Population* (New York: United Nations, 2001); number of women of reproductive age in less developed nations from Population Reference Bureau, op. cit. note 3; United Nations, op. cit. note 4.

36. United Nations Population Division, "Majority of World's Couples Are Using Contraception," UN Release, 20 May 2002; number of women using contraception from UN Population Fund, op. cit. note 34, p. 11; one-quarter and two-thirds of men from ibid., p. 4.

37. Indonesian government declaration from "Government Faces Shortage of Contraceptives for the Poor," *Jakarta Post*, 17 July 2001; increased contraceptive spending needs from Thoraya Obaid, UN Population Fund, opening address at conference on "Meeting the Reproductive Health Challenge: Securing Contraceptives, and Condoms for HIV/AIDS Prevention," Istanbul, 3 May 2001, p. 4.

38. David Achanfuo Yeboah, "Caribbean Countries Pay for Successfully Addressing Population Issues," Population Reference Bureau, April 2002, p. 3. Box 2: Joint UN Programme on HIV/AIDS (UNAIDS), *Report on the Global HIV/AIDS Epidemic* (Geneva: July 2002), pp. 8, 32, 33, 70, 190, and 198; UNAIDS, "Sub-Saharan Africa," fact sheet (Geneva: July 2002); UNAIDS and World Health Organization, *AIDS Epidemic Update December 2001* (Geneva: December 2001), pp. 10, 11, and 22; Karungari Kiragu, "Youth and HIV/AIDS: Can We Avoid Catastrophe?" Population Reports, Series L, No. 12 (Baltimore: The Johns Hopkins University Bloomberg School of Public Health, Population Information Program, Fall 2001), viewed at <www.jhuccp.org/pr/l12edsum .shtml>; David Filipov, "Russia Struggles To Treat AIDS Patients," *Boston Globe*, 21 July 2002, p. A17; WHO, "Women and HIV and Mother-to-Child Transmission," fact sheet, <www.who.int/health-services-delivery/hiv_aids/English/fact-sheet-10/index.html>, viewed 17 May 2002; Center for Health and Gender Equity, "Women at Risk: Why Are STIs and HIV Different for Women?," fact sheet, <www.genderhealth.org/progs/campaign/facts/risk.htm>, viewed 17 May 2002; U.S. Agency for International Development, UNICEF, and UNAIDS, *Children on the Brink 2002* (Washington, DC: July 2002), p. 3; UNICEF, "Orphans and Other Children Affected by HIV/AIDS," fact sheet (New York: February 2002); UNAIDS, "Gender and HIV," fact sheet (Geneva: March 2001); Center for Health and Gender Equity, "Prevention Now: Expanding Access to the Female Condom," fact sheet, <www.genderhealth.org/pubs/prev nowaccess.pdf>, viewed 29 July 2002; Center for Health and Gender Equity, "Frequently Asked Questions About Microbicides," fact sheet, <www.gender health.org/progs/campaign/facts/faqs.htm>, viewed 17 May 2002; World Bank, "HIV/AIDS Blunts Progress in Getting All Children Into School by 2015," press release (World Bank: Washington, DC, 7 May 2002), viewed 20 May 2002.

39. Victoria Brittain, "AIDS Turns Back the Clock for World's Children: 'Shameful statistics' of pandemic and poverty to be laid before UN special session in New York," *The Guardian*, May 4, 2002, p. 23; United Nations, *Report on the Global HIV/AIDS Epidemic* (Geneva: UNAIDS, 2000); Rachel L. Swarns, "Study Says AIDS Is Now Chief Cause of Death in South Africa," *New York Times*, 17 October 2001, p. A5.

40. Noeleen Heyzer, "Women at the Epicentre of the HIV/AIDS Epidemics: The Challenges Ahead," presentation at panel during the UN Special Session on HIV/AIDS, New York, 27 June 2001.

41. World Health Organization, "Gender and Health: A Technical Paper," World Health Organization, 1998, <www.who.int/frh-whd/GandH/Ghreport/gendertech.htm>, viewed 1 August 2002.

42. World Health Organization, "Fourth World Conference on Women Platform for Action, Women and Health," <www.un.org/womenwatch/daw/beijing/platform/health.htm>, viewed 1 August 2002.

43. Michael Paolosso and Sarah Gammage, "Women's Responses to Environmental Degradation: Poverty and Demographic Constraints," *Case Studies From Latin America* (Washington, DC: International Center for Research on Women, 1996), p. 14.

44. Justine Sass, *Women, Men, and Environmental Change: The Gender Dimensions of Environmental Policies and Programs* (Washington, DC: Population Reference Bureau, 2002), p. 3; "Fourth World Conference on Women Platform for Action, Women and Health," <www.un.org/womenwatch/daw/beijing/platform/health.htm>, viewed 1 August 2002.

45. World Health Organization Southeast Asia, "Women's Health in South-East Asia: Women's Health and the Environment," <www.whosea.org/women2/environment.htm>, updated 21 January 2001, viewed 26 April 2002; asthma rates from Women's Environment and Development Organization, *Risks, Rights, and Reforms, A 50-Country Survey Assessing Government Actions Five Years After the International Conference on Population and Development* (New York: WEDO, 1999).

46. UN Food and Agriculture Organization, "Gender and Food Security," <www.fao.org/Gender/en/agri-e.htm>, viewed 18 July 2002.

47. Samanta Sen, "Health-Water: The Killer of 6,000 Children a Day," Inter Press Service wire story, 22 March 2002; Tearfund and WaterAid, *The Human Waste: A Call for Urgent Action To Combat the Millions of Deaths Caused by Poor Sanitation* (London: 2002).

48. Mayling Simpson-Hebert, "Water, Sanitation, and Women's Health: The Health Burden of Carrying Water," World Health Organization, *Environmental Health Newsletter* 25, 1995, cited in Sass, op. cit. note 44, p. 4.

49. Kofi Annan from "Secretary General On Day for Eliminating Violence Against Women, Says Scourge of Gender-Based Violence Must Be Globally Condemned," UN Press Release, 21 November 2000, <www.un.org/womenwatch/daw/news/sg21nov.html>, viewed 1 May 2002 ; Peru from "WHO Says Two in Three Women Abused in Some Countries," *UNWire*, 20 May 2002, <www.unwire.org>; Charlotte Watts and Cathy Zimmerman, "Violence Against Women: Global Scope and Magnitude," *The Lancet*, v. 359, 6 April 2002, p. 1232. Table 2: UN Population Fund, op. cit. note 13, p. 25; female genital mutilation from World Health Organization, "Estimated Prevalence Rates for FGM, Updated May 2001," at <www.who.int/frh-whd/FGM>, viewed 10 November 2001, and from Amnesty International, "Female Genital Mutilation: A Human Rights Information Pack," at <www.amnesty.org/ailib/int cam/femgen/fgm1.htm>, viewed 13 July 2001; rape from Patricia Tjaden and Nancy Thoennes, National Institute of Justice and Centers for Disease Control and Prevention, Research In Brief, November 1998, *Prevalence, Incidence, and Con-*

sequences of Violence Against Women: Findings From the National Violence Against Women Survey (Washington, DC: U.S. Department of Justice, 1998), and from WHO Violence and Injury Prevention, "Violence Against Women: A Priority Health Issue," July 1997, at <www.who.int/_violence_injury_prevention/ vaw/infopack.htm>, viewed 13 November 2001; murders from UNICEF, "Domestic Violence Against Women and Girls," *Innocenti Digest*, May 2000; Molly Moore, "In Turkey, 'Honor Killing' Follows Families to Cities," *Washington Post*, 8 August 2001; Asian Human Rights Commission, "WHO Urges China To Reduce Female Suicides," *Human Rights Solidarity*, January 2000, <www.ahrchk.net/hrsolid/mainfile.php/2000vol10no01/161/>, viewed 1 August 2002.

50.   UN Population Fund, op. cit. note 13, p. 38; Mensch, Bruce, and Greene, op. cit. note 17, p. 46.

51.   Laura Rusu, "Suffering in Silence: The Isolated and Forgotten Victims of Obstetric Fistula," *UN Population News*, 10 May 2002, <www.unfpa.org/news/ 2002/features/fistula.htm>, viewed 1 August 2002.

52.   Rwanda from Valerie Oosterveld, "When Women Are the Spoils of War," *UNESCO Courier*, July/August 1998, <www.unesco.org/courier/1998_08/uk/ ethique/intro.htm>, viewed 1 June 2002; Yugoslavia from Maria Olujic, "Embodiment of Terror: Gendered Violence in Peacetime and Wartime Croatia and Bosnia-Herzegovina," *Medical Anthropology Quarterly*, 1998, v. 12, no. 1, pp. 31-50; West Africa from "Refugee Women's Plight," *New York Times*, 20 June 2002, p. A24.

53.   Suzan Fraser, "Suicides of Women Rising in Traditional Southeast Turkey," *Washington Post*, 9 November 2000, p. A3; Asian Human Rights Commission, op. cit. note 49.

54.   United Nations, op. cit. note 4.

55.   Margaret Greene, personal communication with author, May 2002.

56.   United Nations, "Background Note on the Resource Requirements for Population Programmes in the Years 2000–2015," unofficial white paper, New York, 13 July 1994; *Cairo Programme of Action* <www.iisd.ca/linkages/Cairo/ program/p13007.html>, viewed 1 August 2002.

57.   Commitments at Cairo from Programme of Action, The Programme of Action of the International Conference on Population and Development, <www.undp.org/popin/icpd/conference/ofeng/poa.html>, viewed 23 July 2001; developing-country spending from UN Population Fund, *Financial Resource Flows for Population Activities in 1998* (New York: 1999), p. i; 40 percent from Shanti R. Conly and Shyami de Silva, *Paying Their Fair Share? Donor Countries and International Population Assistance* (Washington, DC: Population Action International, 1998), p. 4.

58.   Barbara Crossette, "UN Agency on Population Blames U.S. for Cut-

backs," *New York Times*, 7 April 2002.

59. Spending goal of $1.9 billion from Shanti R. Conley and Shyami de Silva, *Paying Their Fare Share? Donor Countries and International Population Assistance* (Washington, DC: Population Action International, 1998), p. 82; current spending from Public Policy and Strategic Initiatives Department, PAI, discussion with Robert Engelman, 15 October 2001; gag rule from Richard P. Cincotta and Barbara B. Crane, "The Mexico City Policy and U.S. Family Planning Assistance," *Science*, 19 October 2001, pp. 525–26; U.S. appropriations for HIV/AIDS spending from U.S. Agency for International Development, at <www.usaid.gov/pop_health/aids/Funding/index.html>, viewed 22 September 2001; $500 million figure from Jennifer Loven, "Bush To Propose AIDS Funding Boost; Goal Is To Curb Mother-to-Infant Transmission," 19 June 2002, Associated Press wire story.

60. Religious opposition to contraception from Oscar Harkavy, *Curbing Population Growth: An Insider's Perspective on the Population Movement* (New York: Plenum Press, 1995), pp. 93, 95, 163.

61. Margaret Greene, et al., *In This Generation: Sexual and Reproductive Health Policies for a Youthful World* (Washington, DC: Population Action International, 2002), p.30; Farzaneh Foudi, "Iran's Approach to Family Planning," *Population Today*, July/August 1999, p. 4; United Nations, op. cit. note 2; Mohammad Jalal Abbasi-Shavazi, "Recent Changes and the Future of Fertility in Iran," United Nations Population Division, 2 February 2002, <www.un.org/esa/population/publications/completingfertility/ABBASI paper.pdf>; Allison Tarmann, "Iran Achieves Replacement Level Fertility," Population Reference Bureau, May/June 2002, <www.prb.org/Template.cfm?Sec tion=PRB&template=/Content/ContentGroups/PTarticle/April-June2002/Iran_Achieves_Replacement-Level_Fertility.htm>, viewed 17 July 2002. Figure 6: Data for 1950 through 2000 are from United Nations, *World Population Prospects: The 2000 Revision, Vol. 1* Comprehensive Tables (New York, 2001); data for 2001 from Population Reference Bureau, *2001 World Population Datasheet*, wall chart, <www.prb.org/Content/NavigationMenu/Other_reports/2000-2002/2001_World_Population_Data_Sheet.htm>, viewed 30 July 2002; data for 2002 from U.S. Census Bureau, International Database, <www.census.gov/ipc/www/idbagg.html>, viewed 30 July 2002.

62. "Church Active in Care for Those with AIDS," *Catholic News Service*, 9 July 2001.

63. Central Intelligence Agency, *The World Factbook 2001*, <www.cia.gov/cia/publications/factbook/geos/sp.html#People>, viewed 16 May 2002; "UN Forum on Children Takes Up Abortion; Controversy; Delegates Argue About Whether Phrase Reproductive Health Services Should Be Included in Conference Documents," 9 May 2002, *Los Angeles Times*, p. 3.

64. Marta Lamas, "Standing Fast in Mexico: Protecting Women's Rights in a Hostile Climate," *NACLA Report on the Americas*, March/April 2001, p. 40; David M. Adamson et al., *How Americans View World Population Issues: A Sur-*

vey of Public Opinion (Santa Monica, CA: Rand, 2000), pp. 40, 41, 51, 52.

65. Karen Hardee et al., *Post-Cairo Reproductive Health Policies and Programs: A Comparative Study of Eight Countries*, Policy Papers No. 2 (Washington: The Futures Group International, September 1998); Celia W. Dugger, "Relying on Hard and Soft Sells, India Pushes for Sterilization," *New York Times*, 22 June 2001, p. A1; China from Sophia Woodman, "Draft Law Fails To Address Real Population Issues," *South China Morning Post*, 9 July 2001; India from Rami Chhabra, "Saying Goodbye to Targets," *People & the Planet*, vol. 6, no. 1 (1997), pp. 14–15, from Leela Visaria, Shireen Jejeebhoy, and Tom Merrick, "From Family Planning to Reproductive Health: Challenges Facing India," *International Family Planning Perspectives*, Vol. 25 supplement (1999), pp. S44–49, and from Michael A. Koenig, Gillian H. C. Foo, and Ketan Joshi, "Quality of Care Within the Indian National Family Welfare Programme: A Review of Recent Evidence," *Studies in Family Planning*, March 2000, p. 13.; Juliet Eilperin, "Abortion Issue Stalls UN Family Planning Funds," *Washington Post*, 16 May 2002, p. A6.

66. Mizanur Rahman, Julie DaVanzo, and Abdur Razzaque, "Do Better Family Planning Services Reduce Abortion in Bangladesh?" *The Lancet*, 29 September 2002, pp. 1051-56.

67. Inter-Parliamentary Union (IPU), "Women in National Parliaments," at <www.ipu.org/wmn-e/world.htm>, updated 12 October 2001; IPU, *Women in Parliaments 1945–1995: A World Statistical Survey* (Geneva: 1995); sectors of government from Socorro Reyes, "Getting the Balance Right: Strategies for Change Introduction," at <www.wedo.org/5050/introduction2.htm>, March 2001; Lamas, op. cit. note 64, p. 40.

68. Women's Environment and Development Organization, "Fact Sheet 2: Women Making a Difference," at <www.wedo.org/ fact_sheet_2.htm>, viewed 18 July 2001; IPU, "Women in National Parliaments," op. cit. note 67.

69. Sass, op. cit. note 44, p. 3.

70. UN Population Fund, op. cit. note 13, p. 39; Nigeria, Women's Environment and Development Organization, op. cit. note 45, pp. 17 and 48.

71. Bina Agarwal from International Fund for Agricultural Development, *Rural Poverty Report 2001* (New York: 2001), p. 86, and discussion with Brian Halweil and Danielle Nierenberg, 23 August 2001; World Bank, op. cit. note 19, p. 149.

72. Engelman, op. cit. note 31, pp. 19-21, 34; World Wildlife Fund, *Disappearing Landscapes: The Population/Environment Connection* (Washington, DC: 2001), pp. 16-17, 21-22.

73. Population Action International, *Planting Seeds: New Partnerships for Resource Conservation and Reproductive Health*, Meeting 2001 (Washington, DC: PAI, 2001) pp. 3, 4; John Williams, "Integrating Population Into Environmental Field Projects," *PECS News: A Population, Environmental Change, and Security Newsletter*, The Woodrow Wilson Center, Summer 2001, p. 4.

74. UN Population Fund, op. cit. note 19, p. 51.

75. Engelman, op. cit. note 31, pp. 19–21, 34; Richard E. Benedick, *Human Population and Environmental Stresses in the Twenty-first Century: Environmental Change & Security Project Report* (Washington, DC: Woodrow Wilson Center, 2000), p. 16.

76. Rachel Kyte, Senior Specialist, International Finance Corporation, Washington, DC, discussion with Brian Halweil and Danielle Nierenberg, 26 July 2001.

77. Jodi Jacobson, *Gender Bias: Roadblock to Sustainable Development*, Worldwatch Paper 110 (Washington, DC: Worldwatch, 1992), pp. 47-51.

78. World Bank, op. cit. note 19, pp. 152-154; nations in sub-Saharan Africa from UN Population Fund, op. cit. note 19, p. 41; Lisa C. Smith and Lawrence Haddad, *Overcoming Child Malnutrition in Developing Countries: Past Achievements and Future Choices* (Washington, DC: International Food Policy Research Institute, February 2000), p. 4.

79. Brazil study from World Bank, op. cit. note 19, pp. 152-154; David Dollar and Roberta Gatti, *Gender Inequality, Income, and Growth: Are Good Times Good for Women?* (Washington, DC: World Bank Development Research Group, 1999), pp. 5-6.

80. Jacobson, op. cit. note 77.

81. $17 billion a year figure from Programme of Action of the UN International Conference on Population and Development, <www.iisd.ca/linkages/Cairo/program/p13007.html>, viewed 12 June, 2002; for current status of compliance with the commitments, Summary of the Programme of Action ICPD, <www.cedpa.org/cairo/media/summary.htm>, viewed 12 June 2002; Kofi Annan, *The Flow of Financial Resources for Assisting in the Implementation of the ICPD Programme of Action*, Report of the Secretary-General to the Commission on Population and Development (New York: United Nations Secretariat, February 2001); UN Population Fund, "Coming Up Short: Struggling To Implement the Cairo Programme of Action," <www.unfpa.org/modules/intercenter/upshort/thecairo.htm>, viewed 12 June 2002.

82. Center for Reproductive Law and Policy, *The Bush Global Gag Rule: A Violation of International Human Rights and the US Constitution* (Washington, DC: July 2001), <www.crlp.org/pub_art_ggr.html>, viewed 12 June 2002; The Alan Guttmacher Institute, *The Cairo Consensus: Challenges for U.S. policy at Home and Abroad*, <www.agi-usa.org/pubs/ib4.html>, viewed 1 August 2002.

83. Women's Environment and Development Organization, "Fact Sheet 3: Women in Government, Get the Balance Right" <www.wedo.org/fact_sheet

_3.htm> and "50/50 Get the Balance Right Campaign," <www.unifem-ese asia.org/news/newsMay2001.html#wedo>, viewed 12 June 2002.

84. Save the Children, *State of the World's Mothers 2000*, <www.savethechil dren.org/mothers/pdf/sowm2000.pdf>, viewed 12 June 2002.

85. International Planned Parenthood Federation, "Promoting a New Vision of Masculinity," <www.ippf.org/resource/mbib/>, viewed July 30, 2002; UN Population Fund, op. cit. note 13; Gareth Richards, "We're Not From Mars: Nicaraguan Men Against Violence," <www.panos.org.uk/news/November 2001/Nicaragua_Men_Violence.htm>, viewed 12 June 2002; Ruth Finney Hayward, "Some Organizations Working With Men and Boys To End Violence Against Women and Girls," undated report for the UNICEF Special Project Towards Ending Violence Against Women and Girls, Gender Participation and Partnerships Section, <www.unicef.org/programme/gpp/profiles/pdf/group .pdf>.

86. Population Action International, "Viewpoint: Issue in Focus, How Several Countries Are Successfully Combating HIV/AIDS: The Case of Uganda and Senegal," <www.populationaction.org/news/views/views_issueInFocus _113001a.htm>, viewed 12 June 2002.

87. Center for Reproductive Law and Policy, *Reproductive Rights 2000, Moving Forward, An Overview of the State of Women's Reproductive Rights Worldwide*, (New York, 2000), p. 45.

Index

Other Worldwatch Papers

On Climate Change, Energy, and Materials

157: Hydrogen Futures: Toward a Sustainable Energy System, 2001

151: Micropower: The Next Electrical Era, 2000

149: Paper Cuts: Recovering the Paper Landscape, 1999

144: Mind Over Matter: Recasting the Role of Materials in Our Lives, 1998

138: Rising Sun, Gathering Winds: Policies To Stabilize the Climate and Strengthen Economies, 1997

130: Climate of Hope: New Strategies for Stabilizing the World's Atmosphere, 1996

124: A Building Revolution: How Ecology and Health Concerns Are Transforming Construction, 1995

On Ecological and Human Health

153: Why Poison Ourselves: A Precautionary Approach to Synthetic Chemicals, 2000

148: Nature's Cornucopia: Our Stakes in Plant Diversity, 1999

145: Safeguarding the Health of Oceans, 1999

142: Rocking the Boat: Conserving Fisheries and Protecting Jobs, 1998

141: Losing Strands in the Web of Life: Vertebrate Declines and the Conservation of Biological Diversity, 1998

140: Taking a Stand: Cultivating a New Relationship With the World's Forests, 1998

129: Infecting Ourselves: How Environmental and Social Disruptions Trigger Disease, 1996

On Economics, Institutions, and Security

159: Traveling Light: New Paths for International Tourism, 2001

158: Unnatural Disasters, 2001

155: Still Waiting for the Jubilee: Pragmatic Solutions for the Third World Debt Crisis, 2001

152: Working for the Environment: A Growing Source of Jobs, 2000

146: Ending Violent Conflict, 1999

139: Investing in the Future: Harnessing Private Capital Flows for Environmentally Sustainable Development, 1998

137: Small Arms, Big Impact: The Next Challenge of Disarmament, 1997

On Food, Water, Population, and Urbanization

156: City Limits: Putting the Brakes on Sprawl, 2001

154: Deep Trouble: The Hidden Threat of Groundwater Pollution, 2000

150: Underfed and Overfed: The Global Epidemic of Malnutrition, 2000

147: Reinventing Cities for People and the Planet, 1999

136: The Agricultural Link: How Environmental Deterioration Could Disrupt Economic Progress, 1997

135: Recycling Organic Waste: From Urban Pollutant to Farm Resource, 1997

132: Dividing the Waters: Food Security, Ecosystem Health, and the New Politics of Scarcity, 1996

Other Publications From the Worldwatch Institute

State of the World Library
Subscribe to the *State of the World Library* and join thousands of decisionmakers and concerned citizens who stay current on emerging environmental issues. The *State of the World Library* includes Worldwatch's flagship annual, *State of the World*, plus all five of the highly readable, up-to-date, and authoritative *Worldwatch Papers* as they are published throughout the calendar year.

Signposts 2002
This CD-ROM provides instant, searchable access to over 965 pages of full text from the last two editions of *State of the World* and *Vital Signs*, comprehensive data sets going back as far as 50 years, and easy-to-understand graphs and tables. Fully indexed, *Signposts 2002* contains a powerful search engine for effortless search and retrieval. Plus, it is platform independent and fully compatible with all Windows (3.1 and up), Macintosh, and Unix/Linux operating systems.

State of the World 2002
Worldwatch's flagship annual is used by government officials, corporate planners, journalists, development specialists, professors, students, and concerned citizens in over 120 countries. Published in more than 20 different languages, it is one of the most widely used resources for analysis.

Vital Signs 2002
Written by Worldwatch's team of researchers, this annual provides comprehensive, user-friendly information on key trends and includes tables and graphs that help readers assess the developments that are changing their lives for better or for worse.

World Watch
This award-winning bimonthly magazine is internationally recognized for the clarity and comprehensiveness of its articles on global trends. Keep up to speed on the latest developments in population growth, climate change, species extinction, and the rise of new forms of human behavior and governance.

To make a tax-deductible contribution or to order any of Worldwatch's publications, call us toll-free at 888-544-2303 (or 570-320-2076 outside the U.S.), fax us at 570-322-2063, e-mail us at wwpub@worldwatch.org or visit our website at www.worldwatch.org.

Sources of Data and Information on Gender, Population, and the Environment

The Allan Guttmacher Institute
1120 Connecticut Avenue NW,
    Suite 460
Washington, DC 20036
tel: 202-296-4012; fax: 202-223-5756
e-mail: info@guttmacher.org
website: www.agi-usa.org

Asian-Pacific Resource and Research
    Centre for Women
2nd Floor, Anjung Felda
Jalan Maktab, 54000 Kuala Lumpur
Malaysia
tel: 603-2929913; fax: 603-2929958
e-mail: arrow@arrow.po.my

The Center for Development and
    Population Activities (CEDPA)
1400 16th Street NW, Suite 100
Washington, DC 20036 USA
tel: 202-667-1142; fax: 202-332-4496
e-mail: cmail@cedpa.org
website: www.cedpa.org

Center for Health and Gender Equity
    (CHANGE)
6930 Carroll Ave., Suite 910
Takoma Park, MD 20912
tel: 301-270-1182; fax: 301-270-2052
e-mail: change@genderhealth.org
website: www.genderhealth.org

Center for Reproductive Law and
    Policy
120 Wall Street, 14th Floor
New York, NY 10005
tel: 917-637-3600; fax: 917-637-3666
e-mail: info@crlp.org
website: www.crlp.org

EngenderHealth
440 Ninth Avenue
New York, NY 10001
tel: 212-561-8538; fax: 212-561-8067
e-mail: csvingen@engenderhealth.org
website: www.engenderhealth.org

Family Care International
588 Broadway, Suite 503
New York, NY 10012
tel: 212-941-5300; fax: 212-941-5563
e-mail: info@familycareintl.org
website: www.familycareintl.org

Global Fund for Women
1375 Sutter Street, Suite 400
San Francisco, CA 94109
tel: 415-202-7640; fax 415-202-8604
website:
www.globalfundforwomen.org

International Center for Research
    on Women
1717 Massachusetts Avenue NW,
    Suite 302
Washington, DC 20036
tel: 202-797-0007; fax: 202-797-0020
e-mail: info@icrw.org
website: www.icrw.org

International Planned Parenthood
    Federation
Regent's College
Inner Circle, Regent's Park
London NW1 4NS
United Kingdom
tel: +44 (0)20 7487 7900
fax: +44 (0)20 7487 7950
website: www.ippf.org

International Women's Health
    Coalition
24 East 21st Street
New York, NY 10010
tel: 212-979-8500; fax: 212-979-9009
e-mail: info@iwhc.org
website: www.iwhc.org

National Wildlife Federation
Population and Environment Program
1400 16th Street NW, Suite 501
Washington, DC 20036 USA
fax: 202-797-5486
e-mail: info@nwf.org
website: www.nwf.org

Population Action International
1300 19th Street NW, 2nd Floor
Washington, DC 20036
tel: 202-557-3400; fax: 202-728-4177
website: www.populationaction.org

The Population Council
New York Headquarters
One Dag Hammarskjold Plaza
New York, NY 10017
tel: 212-339-0500; fax: 212-755-6052
e-mail: pubinfo@popcouncil.org
website: www.popcouncil.org

Population Reference Bureau
1875 Connecticut Avenue NW,
  Suite 520
Washington DC 20009-5728
tel: 800-877-9881 or 202-483-1100
fax: 202-328-3937
e-mail: popref@prb.org
website: www.prb.org

Program for Appropriate Technology
  in Health (PATH)
1455 NW Leary Way
Seattle, WA 98107-5136
tel: 206-285-3500; fax: 206-285-6619
e-mail: info@path.org
website: www.path.org

Sierra Club
408 C Street NE
Washington, DC 20002
tel: 202-547-1141; fax: 202-547-6009
website: www.dc.sierraclub.org

United Nations Development Fund
  for Women (UNIFEM)
304 East 45th Street, 15th floor
New York, NY 10017
tel: 212-906-6400; fax: 212-906-6705
e-mail: unifem@undp.org
website: www.unifem.undp.org

United Nations Population Fund
  (UNFPA)
220 East 42nd Street
New York, NY 10017
tel: 212-297-5020; fax: 212-557-6416
website: www.unfpa.org

United Nations Division for the
  Advancement of Women (UNDAW)
2 UN Plaza, DC2-12th Floor
New York, NY 10017
fax: 212-963-3463
e-mail address:daw@un.org
website:
  www.un.org/womenwatch/daw/

Women's Environment and
  Development Organization (WEDO)
55 Lexington Avenue, 3rd Floor
New York, NY 10017-6603
tel: 212-973-0325; fax: 212-973-0335
e-mail: wedo@wedo.org
website: www.wedo.org